# Making Mechanical
# Marvels in Wood

# Making Mechanical Marvels in Wood

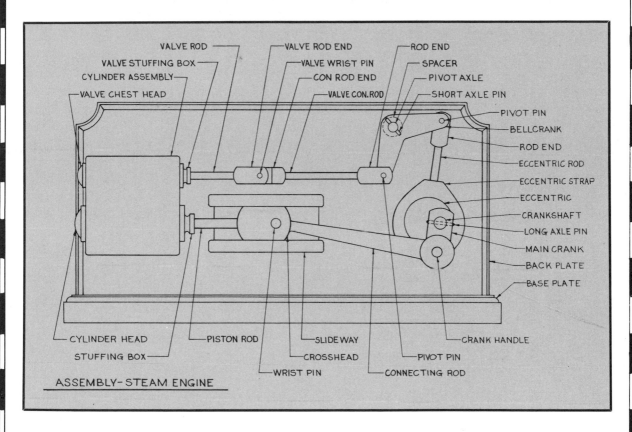

ASSEMBLY-STEAM ENGINE

VALVE ROD
VALVE STUFFING BOX
CYLINDER ASSEMBLY
VALVE CHEST HEAD

VALVE ROD END
VALVE WRIST PIN
CON ROD END
VALVE CON. ROD

ROD END
SPACER
PIVOT AXLE
SHORT AXLE PIN

PIVOT PIN
BELLCRANK
ROD END
ECCENTRIC ROD
ECCENTRIC STRAP
ECCENTRIC
CRANKSHAFT
LONG AXLE PIN
MAIN CRANK
BACK PLATE
BASE PLATE

CYLINDER HEAD
STUFFING BOX
WRIST PIN

PISTON ROD
CROSSHEAD

SLIDEWAY
PIVOT PIN
CONNECTING ROD

CRANK HANDLE

## Raymond Levy

 Sterling Publishing Co., Inc.   New York

# METRIC EQUIVALENCY CHART

MM—MILLIMETRES        CM—CENTIMETRES

## INCHES TO MILLIMETRES AND CENTIMETRES

| INCHES | MM | CM | INCHES | CM | INCHES | CM |
|---|---|---|---|---|---|---|
| ⅛ | 3 | 0.3 | 9 | 22.9 | 30 | 76.2 |
| ¼ | 6 | 0.6 | 10 | 25.4 | 31 | 78.7 |
| ⅜ | 10 | 1.0 | 11 | 27.9 | 32 | 81.3 |
| ½ | 13 | 1.3 | 12 | 30.5 | 33 | 83.8 |
| ⅝ | 16 | 1.6 | 13 | 33.0 | 34 | 86.4 |
| ¾ | 19 | 1.9 | 14 | 35.6 | 35 | 88.9 |
| ⅞ | 22 | 2.2 | 15 | 38.1 | 36 | 91.4 |
| 1 | 25 | 2.5 | 16 | 40.6 | 37 | 94.0 |
| 1¼ | 32 | 3.2 | 17 | 43.2 | 38 | 96.5 |
| 1½ | 38 | 3.8 | 18 | 45.7 | 39 | 99.1 |
| 1¾ | 44 | 4.4 | 19 | 48.3 | 40 | 101.6 |
| 2 | 51 | 5.1 | 20 | 50.8 | 41 | 104.1 |
| 2½ | 64 | 6.4 | 21 | 53.3 | 42 | 106.7 |
| 3 | 76 | 7.6 | 22 | 55.9 | 43 | 109.2 |
| 3½ | 89 | 8.9 | 23 | 58.4 | 44 | 111.8 |
| 4 | 102 | 10.2 | 24 | 61.0 | 45 | 114.3 |
| 4½ | 114 | 11.4 | 25 | 63.5 | 46 | 116.8 |
| 5 | 127 | 12.7 | 26 | 66.0 | 47 | 119.4 |
| 6 | 152 | 15.2 | 27 | 68.6 | 48 | 121.9 |
| 7 | 178 | 17.8 | 28 | 71.1 | 49 | 124.5 |
| 8 | 203 | 20.3 | 29 | 73.7 | 50 | 127.0 |

**Library of Congress Cataloging-in-Publication Data**

Levy, Raymond, 1925–
    Making mechanical marvels in wood / Raymond Levy.
        p.      cm.
    Includes index.
    ISBN 0-8069-7358-7
    1. Woodwork.   2. Models and modelmaking.   3. Mechanical movements.
    I. Title.
    TT180.L438   1991                                91-9634
    621.8—dc20                                       CIP


        1   3   5   7   9   10   8   6   4   2

Copyright © 1991 by Raymond Levy
Published by Sterling Publishing Company, Inc.
387 Park Avenue South, New York, NY 10016
Distributed in Canada by Sterling Publishing
℅ Canadian Manda Group, P.O. Box 920, Station U
Toronto, Ontario, Canada M8Z 5P9
Distributed in Great Britain and Europe by Cassell PLC
Villiers House, 41/47 Strand, London WC2N 5JE, England
Distributed in Australia by Capricorn Ltd.
P.O. Box 665, Lane Cove, NSW 2066
*Manufactured in the United States of America*
*All rights reserved*
Sterling ISBN 0-8069-7358-7

## ACKNOWLEDGMENTS

The inventors of many of the devices in this book lived in the 18th and 19th centuries, and I have included their names, when known. Of contemporary contributors, I must first mention Fiona Wilson of *American Woodworker* magazine, whose superb presentation of my mechanisms in an article brought them to the attention of the publisher of this book. I am grateful to my editor, Michael Cea, who has managed to assemble a book from my material, and to Sean Duggan for his expert color photography. Most of all, I appreciate the contributions of my patient wife, Annette, who consulted on the designs, selected the wood colors, typed the manuscript, and taught music to keep food on the table, so that I could write this book.

Ray Levy
Soquel, California, 1991

# Contents

**Color Section Opposite Page 64**

# Preface

This is a book about wooden mechanisms: what they are, how they work, and how you can make them. In an era when even commonplace items are made of exotic compounds and alloys, it may surprise you to learn that throughout much of the history of civilization most machinery was made of wood. Until the beginning of the Industrial Revolution in 18th-century Britain, when iron became plentiful, large machinery in wind- and water-powered mills was built almost entirely of wood. The wooden gear wheels in many of these mills were five feet or more in diameter, and some were in daily use well into the 20th century. A number of such mills that have been well maintained are still in operation in the Netherlands and in Britain.

Throughout a long career in industry, I designed and built scientific apparatus. Since retirement, I have had a small woodworking shop where I make items to sell. A visit to a San Francisco science museum renewed my interest in apparatus, and I began to build small basic mechanisms for use in classrooms. These mechanisms have become so popular as desk accessories and gift items that my designs have evolved somewhat in those directions.

Some of the models in this collection were designed for this book; some are old friends that I have made for years and have redesigned to improve their appearance and make them easier to build. Most people who see these mechanisms are intrigued with their operation. I hope you will build some of them, and perhaps be inspired to incorporate them into designs of your own.

Ray Levy
Soquel, California 1991

# General Building Guidelines

Although not primarily intended for the beginning woodworker, most of the models in this book should be within the capabilities of the amateur craftsman. The ability to read drawings and the discipline to follow instructions are more important than great skill at woodworking. The dexterity and patience to work on small parts also are essential to successful model-building.

This chapter offers advice on the equipment and material best suited for making the models in this book, as well as helpful sanding and finishing techniques. Before moving on to the projects, read chapter 11, which features workshop aids which will save time and make it easier to build the projects.

## EQUIPMENT

You do not need a lot of equipment to build these models; many of you probably have shops much better equipped than mine. Just about everything in this book can be built with hand tools, and, indeed, I use a lot of them by choice. I would, however, be reluctant to do without my drill press, and a band saw or jigsaw eliminates hours of tedious hand labor. There are many ways to do most jobs, so use what you have, and do the best you can with it.

### The Wagner Safe-T-Planer

If, as I do, you save and use small pieces of rare woods, you will find the Wagner Safe-T-Planer to be an indispensable tool. The distance that the cutting edges project from the solid body of the tool is kept to a minium. This is an important safety feature. Models are sold for use in the drill press or in the radial arm saw. They will safely plane pieces far smaller and thinner than can be managed on any other machine. This is an ideal tool for the woodworker with a very small workshop.

### Drills

For accurately locating holes in woodwork, a small set of good brad-point drills is essential. The best of these have long, slender points and scoring spurs shaped like those on an auger bit. I start all holes with one of these brad-point drills, even though I may complete the drilling with a conventionally ground number- or letter-sized drill, to achieve a desired fit. I have complete sets of drills in fractional inch, letter, and number sizes, and I specify some of each on the various drawings. Large hardware stores sometimes sell individual drills, or you can use the nearest size you have and adjust the diameter of the mating part to fit. There is always a way to do the job, so don't let the lack of a particular tool discourage you.

### The Circle Cutter

This is a very useful tool that is generally not well understood. There are relatively new models on the market with which I have no experience, and to which some of the following may not apply, but most circle cutters sold in the past 40 years are mainly suited for rather thin material. This is because they have always been sold with a single tool bit, ground for hole-cutting only, and with no clearance on its inside edge. This causes a small, continuous deformation of material throughout the cut, generating a lot of heat and side thrust. Illus. 1-1 illustrates the geometry of these tools, and shows how to grind bits properly for disc- or hole-cutting. I routinely cut clean discs from stock up to 1½ inches thick, cutting all the way through from one side. There is no noticeable heat, no splintering, and no roughening of either inside or outside diameter.

Illus. 1-2 shows my larger circle cutter, with several of its tools. Some of these are ground from high-speed-steel lathe-tool bits and some are filed from annealed tool steel, and then hardened, tempered, and ground. The smooth pilot pin is especially useful, as it allows the pilot hole to be drilled with a conventional drill, and eliminates the clogging of the flutes of the short pilot drill supplied with the tool. A lot of the project parts in this book are best made with a circle cutter, so consider obtaining one and learning the proper way to use it.

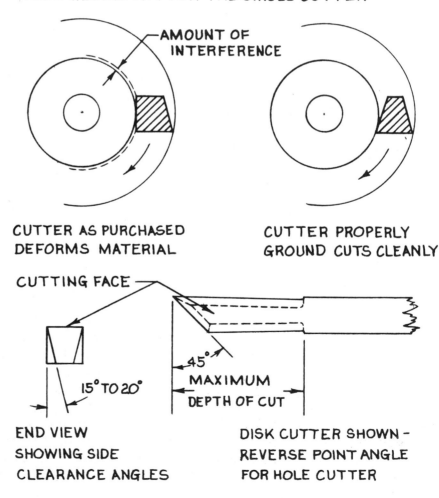

*Illus. 1-1.*

TOOL GEOMETRY FOR THE CIRCLE CUTTER

AMOUNT OF INTERFERENCE

CUTTER AS PURCHASED DEFORMS MATERIAL

CUTTER PROPERLY GROUND CUTS CLEANLY

CUTTING FACE

15° TO 20°

END VIEW SHOWING SIDE CLEARANCE ANGLES

45°

MAXIMUM DEPTH OF CUT

DISK CUTTER SHOWN - REVERSE POINT ANGLE FOR HOLE CUTTER

*Illus. 1-2. From left to right: circle cutter with radius cutter, flat cutter, disk cutter, hole cutter, boring bar, and smooth pilot pin.*

## Circular-Saw Blades

There is on the market today a bewildering profusion of circular-saw blades, domestic and foreign; the manufacturer of each one touts its blade as superior. I own a large and a small carbide-tipped blade. Not being equipped to sharpen these, I use them sparingly, mainly for end-trimming and for template work, where their extra stiffness helps resist deflection.

For most work, I use a conventional rip blade and three identical hollow-ground combination blades, all of carbon steel. I sharpen these several at a time, so I always have a sharp blade available, and am never tempted to use a dull one. The narrow kerfs cut by these hollow-ground blades consume less power and conserve material, compared to the generally thicker carbide-tipped saws. A steel tooth can also be sharpened to a more acute angle than a carbide one, and gives a cleaner cut as a result. A handful of these blades costs only as much as a single sharpening of a carbide-tipped blade.

The sharpening of tools was considered an essential skill when I was an apprentice, and I still consider it to be one today. The geometry of a tool and how it is sharpened can determine the success or failure of even the largest, most expensive machines. Whenever you buy any type of a cutting tool, always consider how you are going to keep it sharp, and factor this into its total cost.

## MATERIAL

Every project part shown in this book is made of hardwood. There are softwoods, such as juniper and red cedar, that are harder than some hardwoods, and these are also suitable. There are two factors to consider when selecting material for one of these projects. The first is appearance; the color of the wood and its grain should be an attractive combination. The other, equally important, factor is the physical properties of the material. Parts that have thin, delicate sections should be made of tough, fine-grained wood that will resist breakage. For moving parts that mesh with others, stability of the material is important. Quite often the harder, denser woods swell and shrink the most when humidity changes. You must either learn about the wood you are using or run your own experiments. When in doubt, allow more clearance.

15

You may notice that my models contain a lot of exotic tropical hardwoods. Many of these are now endangered species, and most of them come from the equatorial rain forests. Therefore, I no longer buy these woods, but use up what I already have.

## DOWELS

Every project in this book uses some dowel stock. Despite advertising claims, I have yet to find a reliable source of accurately sized dowels of good geometry. Some makers advertise sanded dowels, but will admit when questioned that this only applies to dowels with diameters of over ½ inch. Some advertise accuracy within .005 inch, yet deliver rods that are .025 inch out of round. So my advice to you is to buy the best dowels you can find and be prepared to do some work on them.

For reasons stated above, I turn a lot of my own dowel stock on the lathe. I also size some commercial stock by driving it through a series of sharp-cornered holes, of decreasing size, drilled in a steel plate. This works well on some woods, not at all on others.

Illus. 1-3 shows a jig, which is one of several that I use to cut dowels to length. Make the groove just a little deeper than the diameter of the dowel, so you can hold the rod in place with your fingers. Use the finest saw you own; mine has 32 teeth per inch. To make the initial saw cuts in the block, hold a try square so that it will guide the saw, contacting the blade just above the teeth. This won't harm either tool, and will ensure squareness of the cuts.

## SANDING

Do the minimum amount of sanding necessary for each part, but do a good job of it. I prefer to plane and scrape the flat surfaces, but I raise the grain on all parts before applying a finish, and use sandpaper to cut off the "fuzz."

On parts that are inconvenient to plane, I sand with 150- and 240-grit paper, and then switch to a wet-sanding technique. With a hot-air gun plugged in nearby, I dip a small piece of sponge in clean water and wet a piece of 320-grit wet or dry paper. Then I do the following: sand the wood to remove all scratches, clean the paper with a sponge, and wipe any wet-sanding dust off the workpiece with a sponge. Then I wet-sand the piece with 400- and then 600-grit paper, clean the work with a sponge, and quickly dry it with the heat gun. I use a new piece of dry 600-grit paper to cut down any raised grain, and then check the part for scratches with a magnifier. This system works quickly and well, and the waterproof paper is used until it is worn out, instead of being discarded when clogged with resin and wood dust.

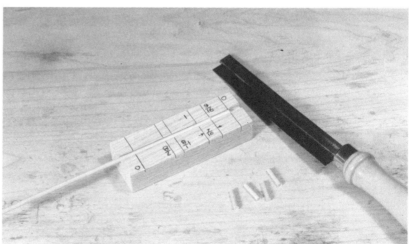

*Illus. 1-3. A cutting jig for five different lengths of ⅛-inch-diameter pins.*

Chapter 11 contains information on how to make an assortment of sanding blocks and sticks that will prove very useful for certain sanding jobs.

## SAFETY TECHNIQUES

The observant reader will notice that many of the photographs depicting a table saw show it being used with no guards in place. Please note: I strongly advocate using guards on machinery, and use them where I can. Unfortunately, most of the small parts for these models simply cannot be made with the guards in the way. One of the least intrusive table-saw guards is the one used by Tage Frid; it consists of a slab of clear acrylic cantilevered over the blade.

I would like to emphasize the importance of safe working habits. Guards will not keep you from harm if you are careless around machinery. You should consider making push sticks. Patterns for my push sticks appear in Illus. 1-4. These push sticks allow you to keep downward pressure on the work and to maintain control of small pieces throughout the sawing operation. I use them all the time. Develop a respectful attitude towards machinery, and you'll discover that it can be used safely.

## FINISHING

A number of factors govern the choice of finishes for these models. Close-fitting parts obviously cannot tolerate finishes that build up films of measurable thickness. On intricately contoured parts and assemblies, it's best to avoid finishes that have to be sanded or rubbed out after they have dried.

The easiest finish to use on these models is one of the various Danish oil finishes sold in most hardware and paint shops. I find it best to paint on a wet coat and wipe it dry almost immediately. If you follow the manufacturer's instructions, allowing 15 minutes for the oil to soak in, you may discover that it will also continue to "bleed" out of the end grain for up to three days, especially on open-pored woods such as red oak.

A few of the mechanisms in this book were finished with a solution of one part of Danish oil to three parts of gloss polyurethane varnish. This is an old finish that seems to be re-invented by someone every few years. The finish is wiped on, rubbed vigorously into the surface, and then wiped quite dry. It requires no sanding or steel wool, and produces an acceptable appearance on most hardwoods with one application.

Most of the models in this book, especially those with very light colored maple structures, were finished with "white" or "clear" shellac. Clear shellac yellows wood less than any other finish with the exception of clear lacquer, which is not suitable. I thin the shellac to "½ pound cut," which simply means ½ pound of shellac flakes to one gallon of alcohol. If the strength of your shellac is not marked on the can, assume that it is a "two pound cut" and thin it with three parts of alcohol to one part of shellac. This finish dries very quickly, so paint a uniform coat on large surfaces, allow it to dry for several hours, and then use steel wool to remove all gloss and any unevenness. On small or complex parts, wipe it on and wipe it dry as quickly as possible, to avoid having to remove the excess finish from tight contours.

Two coats of shellac seem adequate for these models. Shellac produces a nice light-colored finish, but requires more effort than do other materials.

I generally wax these models all over, as they get a lot of handling. Although I have half a dozen waxes on the shelf, both domestic and imported, I prefer Johnson paste wax for these mechanisms. It has the best combination of film strength and slipperiness of any I have tried. Many of the more durable waxes have high coefficients of friction and are better suited for floors than for machinery.

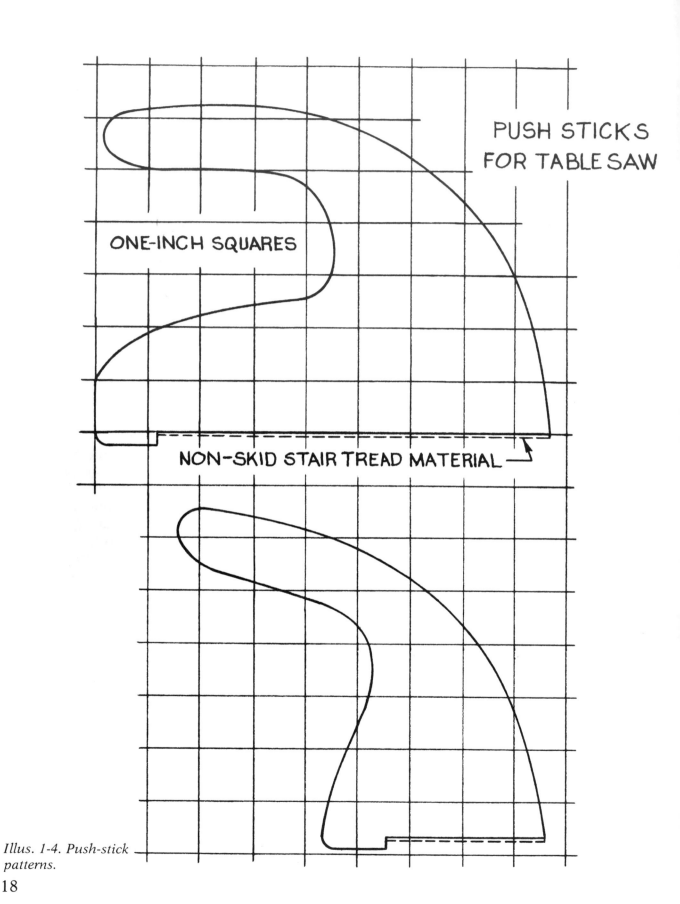

PUSH STICKS
FOR TABLE SAW

ONE-INCH SQUARES

NON-SKID STAIR TREAD MATERIAL

*Illus. 1-4. Push-stick patterns.*

18

# CHAPTER 2

# Basic Mechanisms

The projects in this chapter are mechanical movements that were selected for their interesting actions and because they can be constructed easily in wood. They are fairly easy to build and will give you good experience at fitting and tuning wooden machinery, which will prove extremely helpful when you tackle some of the more complex designs in the book. These five units have a number of similar parts, making it practical to cut parts for all of them at the same time, so why not plan on making the whole set?

Before you begin making any of these projects, or any of the ones that appear later on, study the specific drawings. If you understand the function of each mechanism's part and how it interacts with all of the others, it will help you to prevent problems that can crop up at the final assembly.

## CUTTING THE BACKPLATES AND BASEPLATES

The baseplates are identical for all five units, and the backplates differ only in their hole layouts. (See Illus. 2-1.) To make the backplates, select a piece of hardwood that will have a final width of 5½ inches and thickness of ¾ inch. Joint and plane to these dimensions. Using a clean, sharp blade in the table saw, cut five 3¼-inch pieces from the length of the board. If you clamp a stop block to the saw table, you will be able to cut identical pieces quickly and safely. The purpose in cutting the backs from a wide board, instead of one that matches the 3¼-inch width, is to properly orient the grain for gluing to the base. Throughout this book, on every part drawing where it is needed, the preferred grain direction is indicated by a double arrow on or near the part. Pay attention to these grain directions; they are important.

To make the baseplates, prepare a piece of stock 2¾ inches wide by ¾ inch thick, and cut five 3½-inch lengths from this board. Clean up the saw-cut surfaces on both the backs and bases by sanding them smooth and removing any fuzz.

## DRILL JIG FOR THE BACK-TO-BASE ASSEMBLY

The time you take now to build this drill jig will be well spent because the jig will save

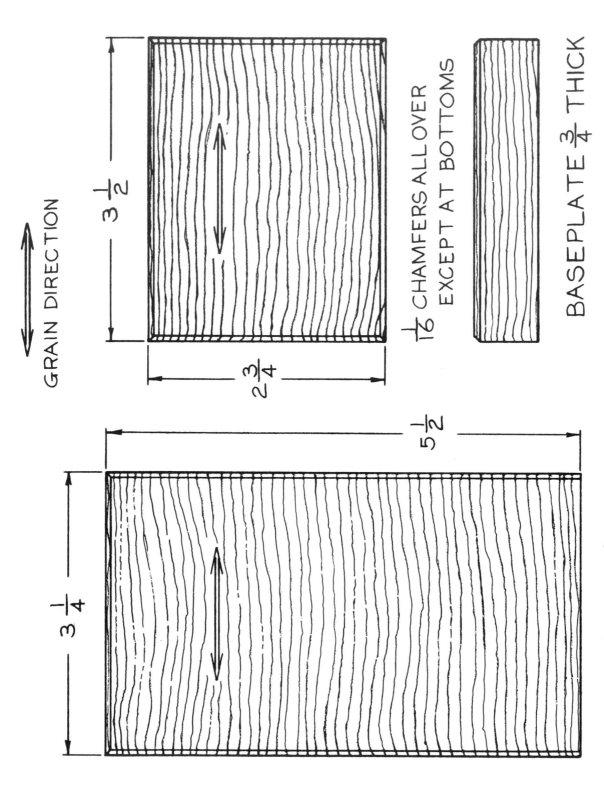

GRAIN DIRECTION

$3\frac{1}{2}$

$2\frac{3}{4}$

$\frac{1}{16}$ CHAMFERS ALL OVER EXCEPT AT BOTTOMS

BASEPLATE $\frac{3}{4}$ THICK

$5\frac{1}{2}$

$3\frac{1}{4}$

BACKPLATE $\frac{3}{4}$ THICK

Illus. 2-1.

20

# DRILL JIG FOR BACK-TO-BASE ASSEMBLY

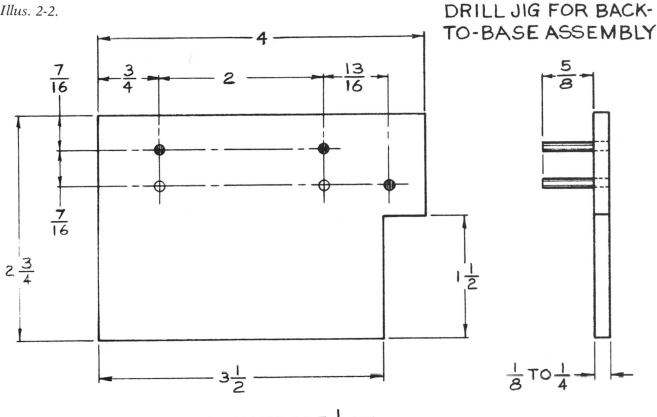

ALL HOLES ARE $\frac{1}{8}$ DIA

DOWELS IN 3 SHADED LOCATIONS

SEE TEXT FOR INSTRUCTIONS

you a considerable amount of time later when you are making the projects. Proper use of this jig will allow you to drill perfectly matched dowel holes in the backplates and baseplates, giving you accurately aligned assemblies.

You can build the jig from Masonite™, hardwood plywood, or good, hard wood that is ⅛ to ¼ inch thick. Cut a piece to 2¾ × 4 inches, and cut the step as shown in Illus. 2-2. Working very accurately, lay out the hole patterns as shown. Drill the five ⅛-inch holes and drive tight-fitting dowels into the three locations indicated; the dowels should be flush with the back of the jig.

To use the jig, place its back flat against the top surface of a baseplate and flush with its rear edge. Align the left and right edges of the jig with the baseplate, and clamp it in place.

(See Illus. 2-3.) If your baseplate is not exactly 3½ inches wide, just center the jig on the part so that the dowel holes will be evenly spaced from both edges. Carefully align the drill with each hole to prevent enlarging the jig, and drill the two holes in the baseplate.

Now, select one edge to be the lower edge of the backplate, and turn it upwards. Set the jig on this bottom surface. The two dowels should touch the back side of the plate, and you should mark the back and front for later reference. The third dowel should touch the edge of the backplate, but, again, if your part is not exactly 3¼ inches wide, just center the holes on the actual width of the plate. Drill the two dowel holes. (See Illus. 2-4.) With holes drilled on all the backs and bases for the dowels, we can now work on the individual mechanisms.

## CAM AND FOLLOWER

A cam is defined as a machine component with a surface whose profile sets in motion another part called the follower in the desired speed and distance. Cams can be made that rotate, reciprocate, or do a combination of both. This model is a rotary cam which has a number of lobes of different heights and spacings, giving a lively action to the follower.

### Making the Parts

The cam, the most difficult part, should be made first. Prepare a piece of sound, uniform stock ½ inch thick. Photocopy the full-size cam pattern in Illus. 2-9 and stick it onto the wood. (See Illus. 2-10.) I use a quick shot of 3-M spray adhesive on the pattern. When I want to remove the paper, I warm it with a heat gun or over my wood stove; the pattern peels right off.

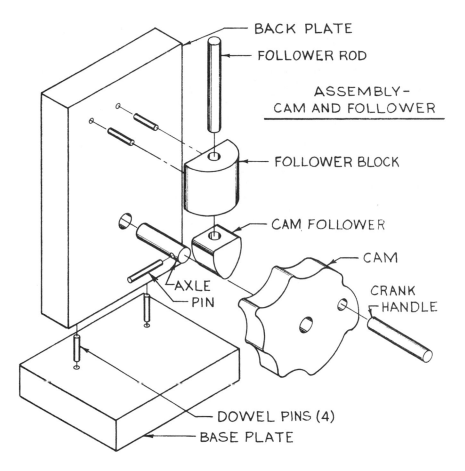

BACK PLATE

FOLLOWER ROD

*Illus. 2-5.*

ASSEMBLY—
CAM AND FOLLOWER

FOLLOWER BLOCK

CAM FOLLOWER

CAM

CRANK
HANDLE

AXLE
PIN

DOWEL PINS (4)

BASE PLATE

*Illus. 2-6. The Cam and Follower mechanism.*

*Illus. 2-7. All the parts for the Cam and Follower mechanism.*

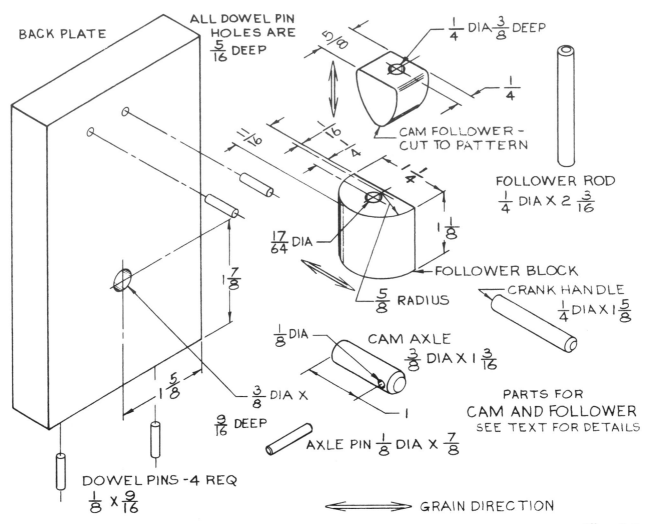

BACK PLATE

ALL DOWEL PIN HOLES ARE $\frac{5}{16}$ DEEP

$\frac{1}{4}$ DIA $\frac{3}{8}$ DEEP

$\frac{5}{8}$

$\frac{1}{4}$

CAM FOLLOWER –
CUT TO PATTERN

FOLLOWER ROD
$\frac{1}{4}$ DIA X 2$\frac{3}{16}$

$\frac{1}{16}$

$\frac{1}{16}$

$\frac{1}{4}$

$1\frac{1}{8}$

$\frac{17}{64}$ DIA

$\frac{5}{8}$ RADIUS

FOLLOWER BLOCK

CRANK HANDLE
$\frac{1}{4}$ DIA X 1$\frac{5}{8}$

$1\frac{7}{8}$

$\frac{1}{8}$ DIA

CAM AXLE
$\frac{3}{8}$ DIA X 1$\frac{3}{16}$

$1\frac{5}{8}$

$\frac{3}{8}$ DIA X

$\frac{9}{16}$ DEEP

1

PARTS FOR
CAM AND FOLLOWER
SEE TEXT FOR DETAILS

AXLE PIN $\frac{1}{8}$ DIA X $\frac{7}{8}$

DOWEL PINS -4 REQ
$\frac{1}{8}$ X $\frac{9}{16}$

GRAIN DIRECTION

*Illus. 2-8.*

Poke an awl into the central point of each hole location, and drill the holes. Check your dowel sizes and refer to the section on drilling in Chapter 1. Note that the hole for the handle does not go all the way through.

When the holes are drilled, set up the band saw with your narrowest blade, and saw out the cam profile as close to the line as is safe. (See Illus. 2-11.) Now, mount a ½-inch-diameter sanding drum in the drill press and sand the cam profile to the line, using a coarse-abrasive sleeve. (See Illus. 2-12.) Switch to a fine-abrasive sleeve and go around the cam again. If you use a thick block on the drill press table as a work support, you can oscillate the drum up and

down while sanding, thereby eliminating all parallel sanding scratches.

For a fine finish, cut a saw slot 3 inches long up one end of a ⅜-inch dowel. Insert one end of a 3-inch-wide strip of 240-grit paper, wrap it around the dowel against the direction of rotation, and anchor it at top and bottom with rubber bands. If you go around the cam with this tool rotating at about 2,000 rpm, the part will acquire a polished surface. Fine-sand the flat faces of the cam and sand a small chamfer all around the profile on each side. Sand off the sharp corners on both sides of the axle hole. Your cam is now completed and should be put somewhere safe to await assembly.

## Cam Follower

This small part, shown in Illus. 2-8, must be carefully made. Like most small parts in these designs, it should be left attached to a larger piece of stock as long as is possible. Square up a block that's ⅝-inch thick and of any width greater than the 13⁄16-inch dimension of the part. Lay out the center of the hole on the end grain and square the center line across the end and down the wide face of the block. Carefully mark the center point of the hole with an awl.

Hold the part in a drill vise or clamp it to a thick block so that it is at right angles in both

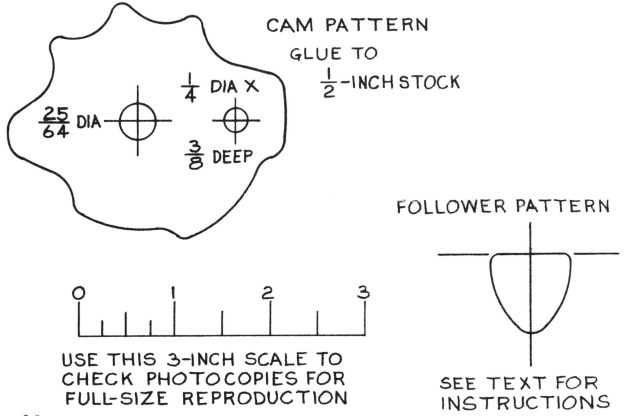

CAM PATTERN
GLUE TO
½-INCH STOCK

$\frac{25}{64}$ DIA

$\frac{1}{4}$ DIA X
$\frac{3}{8}$ DEEP

O    1    2    3

USE THIS 3-INCH SCALE TO
CHECK PHOTOCOPIES FOR
FULL-SIZE REPRODUCTION

FOLLOWER PATTERN

SEE TEXT FOR
INSTRUCTIONS

*Illus. 2-9.*

*Illus. 2-10. The cam patterns glued to the stock.*

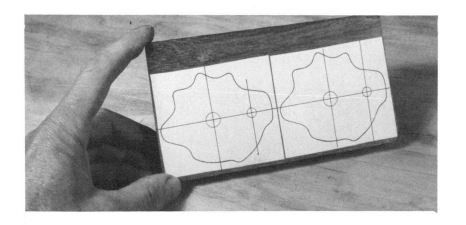

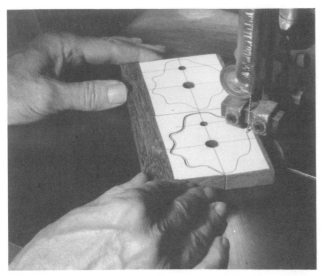

*Illus. 2-11. Cutting out the cams with a band saw.*

*Illus. 2-12. Sanding the contour of the cam.*

*Illus. 2-13. Drilling a hole for the follower rod in the end of the follower blank.*

on its edge and then on its face. If the dowel is visibly not parallel with the test surface either way, it is best to saw off the hole and try again.

Cut out the photocopy of the pattern; leave extra paper around the profile, but cut the straight upper edge exactly on the line. Apply adhesive and stick the pattern to the blank with its upper edge flush with the drilled end of the block and its center line accurately aligned with the center line on the face. Now saw the part to the line with a band saw, removing the part from the longer blank. Put a short length of dowel into the hole to serve as a handle, and belt-sand to the line. Fine-sand by hand, using first 150-grit and then 240-grit paper and sanding with the grain until all the scratches are removed. Lightly chamfer all the edges.

### Follower Block (Illus. 2-8).

Prepare a piece of stock 1⅛ inches wide, ¾ inch thick and long enough to hold onto. Lay out the hole center and the radius center point on one edge. Set a pencil compass to a ⅝-inch radius and draw the semicircular profile of the part. Drill the hole with a ¼-inch brad-point drill and ream it with a 17⁄64-inch regular drill. Check the hole to make

directions to the drill press table. Drill the hole accurately to a ⅜-inch depth with a ¼-inch brad-point drill. (See Illus. 2-13.) Remove the work from the drill press, but don't disassemble the setup until you have made sure that the hole is parallel to the face and the edge. (Drills sometimes wander in end grain.) To do this, put a close-fitting dowel about 4 inches long into the drilled hole, and hold the block against any flat surface, first

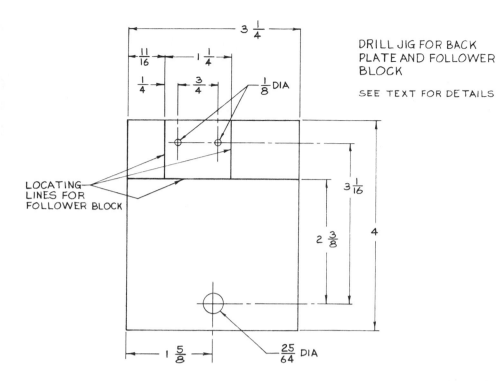

DRILL JIG FOR BACK PLATE AND FOLLOWER BLOCK

SEE TEXT FOR DETAILS

*Illus. 2-14.*

*Illus. 2-15. The follower block clamped to the drill jig.*

*Illus. 2-16. Drilling the dowel pin holes in the follower block, using the flat jig.*

sure that it is parallel to the flat rear face, using the same procedure as with the cam follower. Use a band saw to shape the part, and sand to the line on the belt sander. For all these small parts, the sanding table should be adjusted as close to the belt as possible with-out actually touching it. Hand-sand with the grain and lightly chamfer the curved surfaces only; don't do any sanding on the flat back surface. Chamfer both ends of the hole.

The dowel pin holes in both the follower block and the backplate are located by a simple jig. Cut a piece of thin stock to the dimensions shown in Illus. 2-14, and then lay out and drill the holes. Draw the three locating lines heavy enough to be easily visible.

Align the follower block with the three lines and clamp it with a small padded clamp. (See Illus. 2-15.) Support the jig on two parallel strips, as shown in Illus. 2-16, and drill the dowel holes, 5/16 inch deep. This part is now ready to assemble.

## Backplate and Baseplate

Take one of the backplate blanks and lay out the axle hole center. Drill the hole to the depth shown in Illus. 2-8. Put a short piece of 3/8-inch dowel temporarily into the hole and set the flat drill jig in place. Line up the edges of the jig so that they are parallel with the edges of the plate, and clamp them in place. (See Illus. 2-17.) Drill the two dowel pin holes for the follower block 5/16 inch deep.

Now, sand the backplate to the desired smoothness all over except for the lower edge with the two dowel holes, which should not be sanded. (Also at this time, finish-sand a baseplate.) Finally, plane a uniform chamfer all around, as shown on the drawings. Don't, however, chamfer the lower edge of the back-plate or the lower corners of the baseplate. The backplate and baseplate are now ready for assembly.

## Drill Jig for Axles

Although you can make the parts without this tool, it is very helpful. Drilling accurately centered holes in dowels is never easy. The block jig shown in Illus. 2-18 will drill axles of three different lengths and can be used for four of the mechanisms, so it is worth your time to make one.

Square up a block of the hardest wood available and scribe the hole centers as shown in Illus. 2-18. Work carefully; the parts you drill in any jig will never be any more accurate than the jig itself. Drill the large central hole from both ends, using first an undersize drill, and then drilling all the way through with the final drill. Put a piece of scrap dowel in the 3/8-inch hole before drilling all the 1/8-inch holes, to prevent splintering. Number the stop-pin holes as shown in Illus. 2-18, as they will be referred to by number from now on. Insert the parts into the jig and hold them against the stop pin by applying thumb pressure on the exposed end. (See Illus. 2-19.)

*Illus. 2-17. Drilling dowel holes for the follower block, with the flat jig clamped to the backplate.*

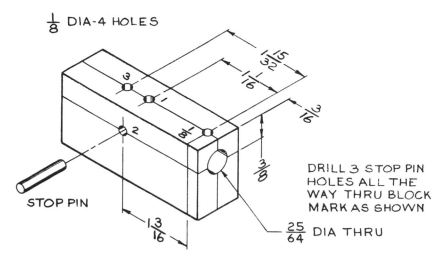

$\frac{1}{8}$ DIA-4 HOLES

STOP PIN

DRILL 3 STOP PIN
HOLES ALL THE
WAY THRU BLOCK
MARK AS SHOWN

$\frac{25}{64}$ DIA THRU

AXLE DRILL JIG
USED ON 4 DIFFERENT PROJECTS
SEE INSTRUCTIONS

*Illus. 2-19. A jig for drilling the pin holes in the axles.*

## Remaining Parts

The rest of the pieces of this assembly, shown in Illus. 2-8, are all made from dowels. The crank handle is used in four of the five models, and the axle pin in three of them, so you may as well cut all of them at once. Cut them to length with a fine-toothed handsaw and chamfer the ends in the lathe or by sanding. Those parts that will be glued in place should be snugly hand-fitted into their respective holes. These parts will swell the moment they are wetted with glue, so if they are very tight to begin with you may not be able to fully insert them before they lock in place.

Parts intended for running fits should have about 1/64-inch clearance in their holes. This is about the minimum desirable clearance for wooden assemblies if you want the machine to function when the humidity changes. Sand all the parts with fine abrasive, finishing parallel to the grain.

Push-fit the 1/8-inch axle pin into the axle. This is the last piece to be assembled, and you don't want to hammer it in. Use the jig with the stop pin in the number one hole to drill a hole in the axle for the pin.

## Dry-Assembling the Mechanism

At this point, with all the parts completed, dry-assemble the mechanism. Put two dowels into their holes in the follower block and mount the block onto the backplate. Place the axle into its hole in the backplate. Now, push the follower rod into the cam follower; it should enter the bottom of its hole without requiring a great deal of force.

Slide the rod into its guide hole in the follower block; the assembly is so designed that the follower will just clear the axle when

29

everything is correctly made. If there is any interference, check the length of the follower rod; it may be a bit too long. When you have the follower in place, push it all the way up and check its clearance to the backplate. This clearance should be about 1/64 inch. Much less than that, and the follower may hang up. Much more will give a wobbly action. Remember that the follower returns by gravity and must fall of its own weight.

Assemble the cam on the axle and put the handle temporarily in place. With the backplate in an upright position, test the operation of the assembly. When the cam is turned in a clockwise direction, the follower should rise and fall with a smooth positive action; it will work more smoothly when finished and waxed.

If the follower is reluctant to climb any of the lobes on the cam, the chances are that you have undercut the contour and made a steep angle of rise on that lobe. The way to fix this is to slightly reduce the angle of the lobe until the action is acceptable. This should never occur if you work reasonably close to the template outline.

Put two dowels into the holes in the base and set the backplate in position, to see that it can be assembled correctly.

Take everything apart and refer to the section on wet-sanding in Chapter 1. When the parts are smooth enough to suit you, proceed with the assembly.

## Final Assembly

Prepare the gluing surfaces of the backplate and baseplate, by lightly scraping them with a sharp scraper. Push two dowels into the holes in the baseplate. You don't have to put glue into these holes, as the dowels only position the parts and don't contribute to the structural strength.

Apply a film of glue to both surfaces and set the backplate in place. Make sure that the axle hole is at the front of the unit (I once glued one backwards). Pull the assembly tight, using one large clamp with a couple of

small wood pads to protect the work. With a small square, check the assembly. If the backplate leans to the front or the rear, slightly loosen the clamp and push one of its jaws in the right direction to correct this condition. When you have determined that the assembly is squared up, set it aside to dry. (See Illus. 2-20.)

*Illus. 2-20. Gluing the backplate to the baseplate.*

Lightly scrape the gluing areas and assemble the follower block onto its dowels. Use a clamp with a piece of cardboard attached to it to prevent the curved surface of the part from being crushed, and glue the block in place. When this assembly is dry, wipe a thin film of glue around the inside of the axle hole in the backplate; use only a little glue so that it doesn't fill the hole. Put a long piece of 1/8-inch dowel or a metal rod in the pin hole of the axle. Put the axle through the cam, and start its end into the hole in the backplate. Keeping the long 1/8-inch dowel reasonably horizontal, tap the axle into its hole until the pin hole with its long dowel is about 1/32 inch from the face of the cam; more clearance here is better than less. (See Illus. 2-21.) Remove the long dowel and the cam. Glue the crank handle into the cam, and the follower rod into the follower. This completes the gluing.

Clean up the assembly. Before adding a finish, read the section on finishing; the choice of finishes is important. When you have applied a finish to all the subassemblies, work a little wax into the holes in the follower block and the cam. A pipe cleaner is ideal for this purpose. Also wax the follower rod, the axle, and the contours of the cam and follower, and buff off any excess wax. You may wax all other surfaces if you wish. Slide the follower into position, and put the cam on its axle. Push the axle pin into its hole and center it; don't glue this pin. Operate this assembly. There should be a lively clip-clop sound when it is rotated rapidly which will fascinate your family and friends.

Congratulations! You have just built a functioning, all-wooden mechanism.

# THE ECCENTRIC

If you took a conventional crankshaft and greatly enlarged its crankpin, you would have what is commonly called an eccentric. (See Illus. 2-22–2-24.) An eccentric is preferred wherever the need for a very short stroke makes it impractical to use a regular crankshaft. Its very large bearing area makes the eccentric ideal for high-load applications; heavy presses are usually actuated by large eccentrics. Other such applications include high-pressure piston pumps and steam engine valve gear.

## Making the Parts (Illus. 2-25)

Our model has two main parts that must be fitted together with the proper clearance: the eccentric and the eccentric strap. The order in which you should make these parts depends on the equipment available to you. If you own an adjustable circle cutter, then it doesn't matter which of the two parts you make first. Otherwise, it is best to cut the hole in the eccentric strap, and then fit the eccentric to it.

To make the eccentric strap, plane a sound piece of stock to a 1/2-inch thickness, and glue on the pattern, which is shown in Illus. 2-27. Using a brad-point drill of the same diameter as the pilot drill in your circle cutter, put a hole in the center of the pattern. (See Illus. 2-26.) This is a surer way to produce an accurately centered hole than attempting to do it with the short, blunt drill in the circle cutter. I substitute a polished piece of steel

*Illus. 2-21. Assembling the axle.*

*Illus. 2-22.*

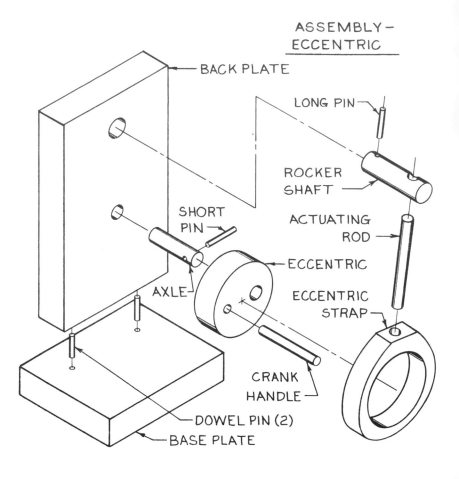

BACK PLATE

LONG PIN

ROCKER
SHAFT

SHORT
PIN

ACTUATING
ROD

ECCENTRIC

AXLE

ECCENTRIC
STRAP

CRANK
HANDLE

DOWEL PIN (2)

BASE PLATE

*Illus. 2-23. The Eccentric.*

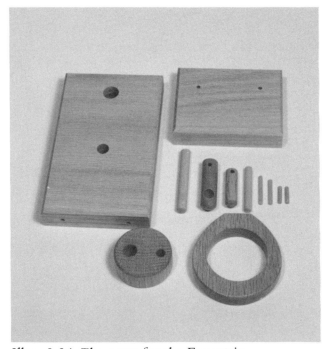

*Illus. 2-24. The parts for the Eccentric.*

32

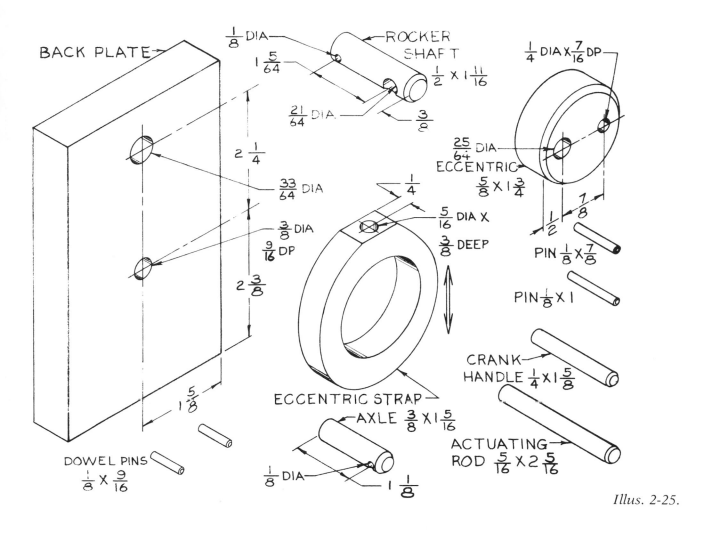

BACK PLATE

ROCKER SHAFT

$\frac{1}{8}$ DIA

$1\frac{5}{64}$

$\frac{21}{64}$ DIA

$\frac{3}{8}$

$\frac{1}{2} \times 1\frac{11}{16}$

$\frac{1}{4}$ DIA X $\frac{7}{16}$ DP

$\frac{25}{64}$ DIA

ECCENTRIC

$\frac{5}{8} \times 1\frac{3}{4}$

$2\frac{1}{4}$

$\frac{33}{64}$ DIA

$\frac{3}{8}$ DIA

$\frac{9}{16}$ DP

$2\frac{3}{8}$

$\frac{1}{4}$

$\frac{5}{16}$ DIA X

$\frac{3}{8}$ DEEP

$\frac{1}{2}$

$\frac{7}{8}$

PIN $\frac{1}{8} \times \frac{7}{8}$

PIN $\frac{1}{8} \times 1$

CRANK HANDLE $\frac{1}{4} \times 1\frac{5}{8}$

ECCENTRIC STRAP

AXLE $\frac{3}{8} \times 1\frac{5}{16}$

ACTUATING ROD $\frac{5}{16} \times 2\frac{5}{16}$

$1\frac{5}{8}$

DOWEL PINS $\frac{1}{8} \times \frac{9}{16}$

$\frac{1}{8}$ DIA

$1\frac{1}{8}$

*Illus. 2-25.*

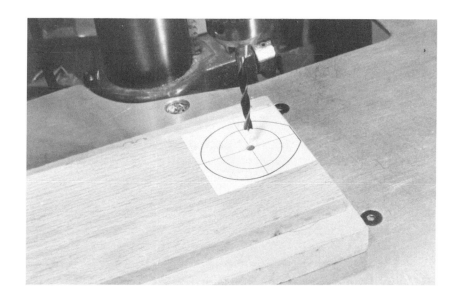

*Illus. 2-26. Drilling the pilot hole in the Eccentric strap. See the following page for the full-size pattern.*

33

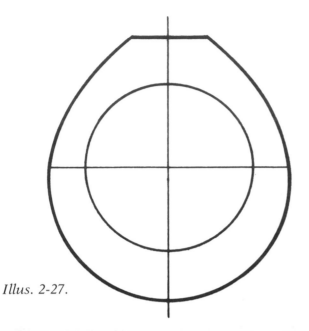

Illus. 2-27.

PATTERN FOR

## ECCENTRIC STRAP

TRACE OR PHOTOCOPY

GLUE TO $\frac{1}{2}$ INCH STOCK

0    1    2

USE THIS INCH SCALE
TO CHECK SIZE OF
PHOTOCOPY

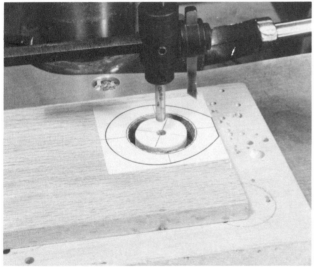

Illus. 2-28. Cutting the 1¾-inch central hole in the Eccentric.

Illus. 2-29. Setting the centerline on the pattern square with the drill press table.

rod for the pilot drill whenever I do this kind of operation.

Bore a trial hole in a test piece if you already have made the eccentric. Otherwise, just cut the hole to the drawing dimension and make the eccentric to fit. If you have the eccentric, then bore a hole to give it a clearance of at least ¹⁄₆₄ inch, but not more than ¹⁄₃₂ inch. (See Illus. 2-28.)

Remove the work from the drill press, cut out the outer profile with a band saw, and sand it, but don't remove the paper pattern just yet. Square the center line of the pattern across the flat upper end of the part, and lay out the center of the hole for the actuating rod. Secure the part in a drill vise or clamp it to a block, setting the center line on the face of the pattern square with the drill press

34

table. (See Illus. 2-29.) Next, drill the rod hole. Now, remove the paper pattern, round the corners of the curved contour, and sand the part.

If you don't own a circle cutter, there are several other ways that you can make this part. A hole saw can be used; you will probably have to use a sanding drum to smooth the hole's surface. You can also saw out the circle with a jigsaw or even a coping saw, and drum-sand to the line. These loosely fitted parts do not need precise circles.

The eccentric is best made as a slice off a round rod. This produces a part with the end grain on its flat faces, and one that has the best chance for remaining circular when the humidity changes. If you don't own a lathe and can't get 1¾-inch rod, just cut a ⅝-inch-thick slab off the end of a piece of 1¾-inch-thick stock, lay out the circle, and saw and sand the slab to size. The least desirable alternative is to cut the disk from flat stock, preferably quarter-sawn.

Fit the eccentric into the hole in the eccentric strap, allowing a 1/64-inch-minimum clearance. Illus. 2-30 shows parts cut from a rod and sawn from a slab, and a stack of three parts turned in a lathe.

Lay out and drill the axle and crank handle holes; remember that the handle hole goes only part of the way through. Hand-sand the outside diameter in the direction of rotation,

sanding through 240-grit or finer paper. If you make the part on a lathe, a large chamfer on the outer face will enhance its appearance. Otherwise, hand-sand or file a small chamfer.

The rocker shaft is used on two of the five mechanisms, so you might consider making the simple block jig for drilling the holes. (See Illus. 2-32.) Illus. 2-31 shows all its dimensions. This jig is made like the axle jig. Hold the part against the stop pin in the jig, and drill the 21/64-inch hole. Put a short piece of 5/16-inch dowel through the jig and the part, and drill the ⅛-inch hole. This way both holes will be aligned, which does not make the part work any better, but certainly makes it look better. Chamfer both ends of the shaft to the drawing dimensions, using a lathe or by belt- or disk-sanding.

Make the actuating rod, the crank handle, and the axle. Drill the axle using the jig with its stop pin in hole number 2. (See Illus. 2-18.) Cut the long and short axle pins, and sand each so that you can use your thumb to push-fit it into its hole. Then make two small dowel pins for the back-to-base assembly.

Take one of the backplate blanks and, checking that the two dowel pin holes are on the bottom edge, lay out the two hole centers on the front face. Drill the axle hole to depth, and the rocker shaft hole all the way through. You probably don't own a 33/64-inch drill and won't want to buy one, so cut a 3-inch-long

*Illus. 2-30. Three methods of making an Eccentric. The piece on the left was cut from a rod. The piece in the middle was sawn from an end-grain slab. The three pieces on the right were turned on a lathe.*

35

*Illus. 2-31.*

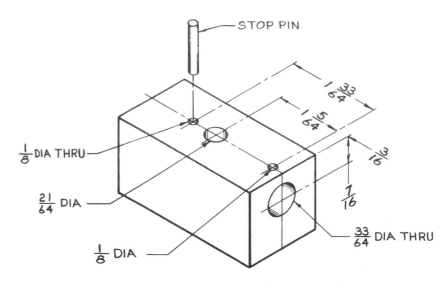

STOP PIN

$1\frac{33}{64}$

$1\frac{5}{64}$

$\frac{9}{16}$

$\frac{1}{16}$

$\frac{1}{8}$ DIA THRU

$\frac{21}{64}$ DIA

$\frac{33}{64}$ DIA THRU

$\frac{1}{8}$ DIA

DRILL JIG FOR ROCKER SHAFT

*Illus. 2-32. This drill jig is used to make the rocker shaft for the Eccentric and the Self-Conjugate Cam.*

*Illus. 2-33. Sanding the rocker-shaft hole to size.*

slot on a ⅜-inch dowel, anchor a piece of 100-grit paper into the slot, and, turning the rod in the direction of rotation, wind on enough sandpaper to just fill the drilled hole. Run this tool at a fairly low speed, below 1,000 rpm, while oscillating it up and down. You will have the desired fit for your rocker shaft in a short time. (See Illus. 2-33.) This

hole sander is a handy tool that I make in various sizes to smooth or enlarge holes where needed.

Lightly chamfer the large hole, front and back, and fine-sand the part; chamfer the corners last. Also, sand and chamfer one of the baseplates. Now, make a dry assembly of all the parts to check fits and clearances.

## Assembling the Mechanism

Fine-sand all the parts, raising the grain if necessary. Glue the backplate to the base-plate, checking for squareness as outlined in the cam and follower instructions. Glue the actuating rod into the eccentric strap, checking against a flat surface to be sure that the rod is parallel to the face of the part. Put a long dowel into the axle pin hole to assist in keeping the hole level, and put the axle through the eccentric. Wipe a little glue around the inside of the axle hole, put the axle into the hole, and tap it in until the long rod is 1/32 inch from the face of the eccentric. Glue the crank handle into the eccentric. (See Illus. 2-24.)

Apply a finish to all the parts, and when they are dry, wax all the sliding surfaces. Place the eccentric on its axle and push in the shorter of the two axle pins, centering it neatly. Put the slide rod through its hole in the rocker shaft, and simultaneously slide the shaft into its hole and the eccentric strap onto the eccentric. Push in the long axle pin behind the plate. You can now try your mechanism and show it to the neighbors.

## SCOTCH YOKE (ILLUS. 2-34–2-36)

The third unit in this group is an example of the pin-and-slot mechanism known to steam-engine enthusiasts as the Scotch Yoke. The use of this design eliminates the need for the conventional connecting rod found in most engines, and results in a very compact mechanism. Its somewhat greater mass limits the Scotch Yoke to slow-running applications, but it was used a great deal on small marine steam engines and on reciprocating pump drives. Various versions of this mechanism are often used in industrial equipment designs.

*Illus. 2-34.*

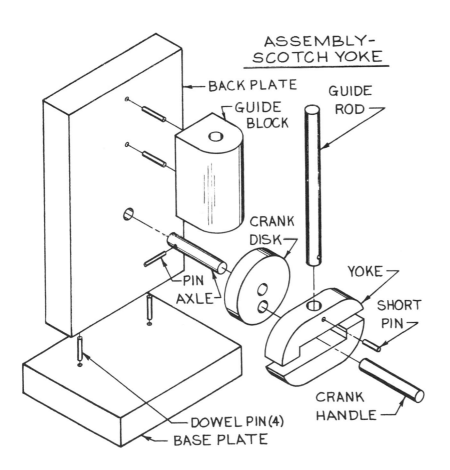

ASSEMBLY-
SCOTCH YOKE

BACK PLATE

GUIDE
BLOCK

GUIDE
ROD

CRANK
DISK

PIN
AXLE

YOKE

SHORT
PIN

CRANK
HANDLE

DOWEL PIN (4)
BASE PLATE

Illus. 2-35. The Scotch Yoke.

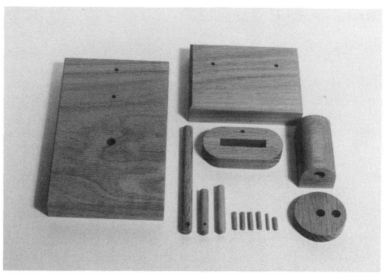

Illus. 2-36. All the parts for the Scotch Yoke.

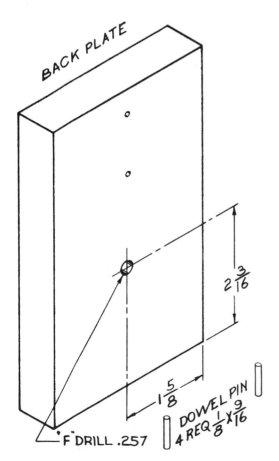

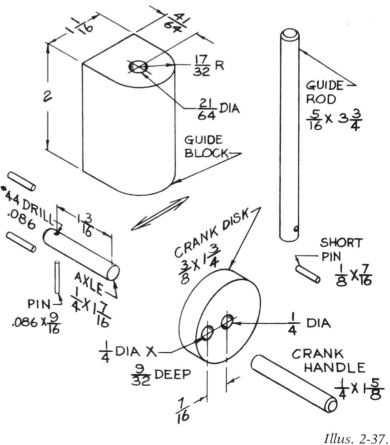

BACK PLATE

$2\frac{3}{16}$

$1\frac{5}{8}$

F DRILL .257

DOWEL PIN
4 REQ $\frac{1}{8}$ X $\frac{9}{16}$

GUIDE BLOCK

$1\frac{1}{16}$

$\frac{41}{64}$

2

$\frac{17}{32}$ R

$\frac{21}{64}$ DIA

GUIDE ROD
$\frac{5}{16}$ X $3\frac{3}{4}$

SHORT PIN
$\frac{1}{8}$ X $\frac{7}{16}$

#44 DRILL
.086

$1\frac{3}{16}$

AXLE
$\frac{1}{4}$ X $1\frac{7}{16}$

PIN
.086 X $\frac{9}{16}$

CRANK DISK
$\frac{3}{8}$ X $1\frac{3}{4}$

$\frac{1}{4}$ DIA

$\frac{1}{4}$ DIA X
$\frac{9}{32}$ DEEP

$\frac{1}{16}$

CRANK HANDLE
$\frac{1}{4}$ X $1\frac{5}{8}$

Illus. 2-37.

38

## Making the Parts (Illus. 2-37)

The backplate has only a single axle hole and two small dowel pin holes in its front surface. It is important in this design that the axle fits properly into its bearing hole, so test your dowel stock to be sure that you have selected the best available size drill. A letter F drill drills a diameter of .257 inch, which is exactly halfway between 1/4- and 17/64-inch, and usually makes a nice running fit for a 1/4-inch-diameter rod. Holes for the two small dowel pins are located in both the backplate and the guide block by means of the flat drill jig shown in Illus. 2-40, which ensures proper placement of the block.

The guide block is made from a thick piece of stock whose grain must run across the part, as shown in Illus. 2-37. If you can't get thick material, glue two thinner pieces to make the block, but make certain that the joint does not run through the guide rod hole. Lay out the center and radius of the hole on each end of the block, drill halfway through from both ends using a 1/4-inch brad-point drill, and finish by drilling with a 21/64-inch drill all the way through from one side. (See Illus. 2-41.) Check that this hole is parallel to the back face of the block. Saw and sand the

radius to the line, fine-sanding by hand parallel to the direction of the grain. Center the block in the lines on the drill jig, clamp it in place, and drill the two dowel pin holes 5/16 inch deep.

Machine the two halves of the yoke across the end of a wide board and cut them off after the work is completed. I use a wide enough piece of stock to get several sets of parts from it. Saw out the step and smooth its surface, if necessary, using a fine file. (See Illus. 2-43.) Do all necessary smoothing of this surface before slicing the block into individual parts, as these will be small pieces and difficult to work on. The depth of the step should be about 1/64 inch greater than the diameter of the dowel you will be using for the crank handle; more clearance won't matter, but too little may cause the device to bind at the top and bottom of the stroke, especially if your crankshaft is a little loose in its bearing.

When you are satisfied with the quality of this step, cut the end off the board (Illus. 2-44), set the rip fence the correct distance from the blade, and cut the piece into individual yoke parts (Illus. 2-45). Make sure that you use a push stick, as described in the equipment section. Don't get your fingers anywhere near the blade.

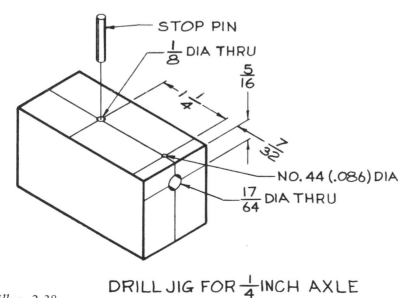

DRILL JIG FOR 1/4 INCH AXLE

*Illus. 2-38.*

*Illus. 2-39. This drill jig is used to drill a pin hole for a 1/4-inch-diameter axle.*

39

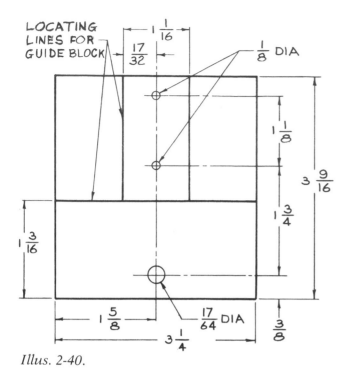

$1\frac{1}{16}$

$\frac{17}{32}$

$\frac{1}{8}$ DIA

$1\frac{1}{8}$

$3\frac{9}{16}$

$1\frac{3}{4}$

$1\frac{3}{16}$

$1\frac{5}{8}$

$\frac{17}{64}$ DIA

$\frac{3}{8}$

$3\frac{1}{4}$

*Illus. 2-40.*

*Illus. 2-41. The guide block with the hole drilled.*

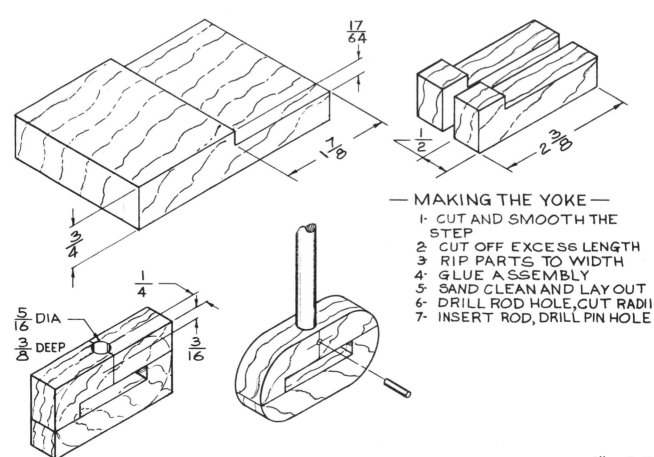

$\frac{17}{64}$

$1\frac{7}{8}$

$\frac{3}{4}$

$\frac{1}{2}$

$2\frac{3}{8}$

$\frac{5}{16}$ DIA

$\frac{3}{8}$ DEEP

$\frac{1}{4}$

$\frac{3}{16}$

## — MAKING THE YOKE —

1. CUT AND SMOOTH THE STEP
2. CUT OFF EXCESS LENGTH
3. RIP PARTS TO WIDTH
4. GLUE ASSEMBLY
5. SAND CLEAN AND LAY OUT
6. DRILL ROD HOLE, CUT RADII
7. INSERT ROD, DRILL PIN HOLE

*Illus. 2-42.*

*Illus. 2-43. The first step in making the yoke.*

*Illus. 2-44. The end of the blank cut off to the length of the finished parts.*

*Illus. 2-45. On the left is the blank. In the middle are the three parts cut off a blank. On the right is the push stick used to make this cut.*

*Illus. 2-46. Gluing the yoke assembly.*

*Illus. 2-47. The yoke sanded clean and laid out.*

Check that the two yoke halves fit well together, and glue them as shown in Illus. 2-46, clamping lightly. Remove any squeezed-out glue from inside the yoke before it has a chance to harden. Let the glue get quite gummy, and use a narrow knife blade to remove it from the slot.

When the joints have dried, sand the two flat faces, lay out the two large radii, and saw and sand to shape. Lay out the center of the guide rod hole, and square its center line

down the front face of the yoke. Mark the center of the pin hole. (See Illus. 2-47.) Check the actual size of your 5/16-inch dowel stock, and select a drill that will drill a hole into which it will fit snugly. Drill the guide rod hole in the yoke to the depth shown, taking care that the drill point doesn't break through into the slot. Sand the guide rod if necessary to achieve a snug fit, keeping in mind the fact that this part must be inserted last of all at assembly, and should not be hammered in.

Push the rod into the yoke, and drill the 1/8-inch pin hole through both parts. (See Illus. 2-48.) Remove the rod, without allowing it to turn, and make a pencil dot just below the pin hole. Now, make a pencil mark inside the 5/16-inch hole, and you will be able to assemble the parts in the same orientation as when they were drilled.

*Illus. 2-48. Drilling the pin hole in the yoke and the rod.*

Next, make the crank disk from 3/8-inch-thick stock. I use a circle cutter with its disk-cutting tool bit; the parts require only light finish-sanding. You can also saw out the part or turn it on the lathe. Lay out the crank handle hole and drill to depth, keeping the hole as square as possible with the face.

Make the remaining dowel parts: the crank handle, the axle, the two small pins, and the four ⅛ × ⁹⁄₁₆-inch dowel pins. The axle should be a close fit in its bearing hole in the backplate. It must also fit snugly into the center hole of the crank disk, but not too tightly, because you have to adjust it while gluing the parts.

A hole must be drilled into the axle for its little pin. I use round toothpicks that are very close to .086 inch in diameter. This corresponds to the size of a number 44 drill, which is what I use to drill the axle. I shave the pins to size by pushing the toothpicks through a sharp-cornered hole drilled in a piece of steel with a number 44 drill. To make one or two pins, you can just sand them so that they can be push-fitted into their axles.

The drill jig for the axle hole, shown in Illus. 2-38 and 2-39, and the cutting jig for the small pins, shown in Illus. 2-49 and 2-50, can be used on several of the mechanisms if you want to make them. If you build these jigs now, they will make it easier to build the mechanisms later on.

The retaining pin for the guide rod should be exactly ⁷⁄₁₆ inch long or slightly shorter. If the pin is even a little too long, you may not be able to disassemble the mechanism. To disassemble the mechanism, position the crank handle at top center and drive in the short pin until the guide rod can be wiggled out of its hole. The yoke is now free, and the pin can be removed for reassembly. If you

*Illus. 2-49.*

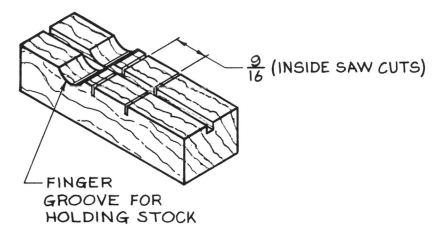

$\frac{9}{16}$ (INSIDE SAW CUTS)

FINGER GROOVE FOR HOLDING STOCK

## JIG FOR CUTTING AXLE PINS
### (FROM TOOTHPICKS)

*Illus. 2-50. Axle-pin cutting jig.*

make the pin too long, it will hit the backplate before it clears the guide rod, and you will have to resort to surgery to remove it.

When all parts are completed, assemble the components. Start with the axle-to-disk assembly. Working quickly, put a film of glue inside the axle hole in the disk and place the axle into the hole. Insert the axle through the backplate and immediately tap it into the disk until the small pin hole is about $\frac{1}{64}$ inch from the backplate. (Now you see why these parts should not be fitted together too tightly before gluing.)

Let this joint dry. Then sand the end of the axle flush with the front of the disk and finish-sand the disk. If you pad the axle with thin cardboard and hold it in a drill chuck, you can sand the diameter and corners of the disk while it is rotating, which is a quick way to get a smooth, finish-sanded part. Glue the crank handle into its hole in the disk, and check carefully to be sure it is square to the surface in all directions.

Put two dowel pins into the holes in the backplate and set the guide block in place. Make a trial assembly of all parts, and test their operation. Make sure that there is clearance between the flat face of the yoke and the crank disk. There should be just enough clearance for the unit to move freely, but not enough for the yoke to swivel noticeably while operating. Try the yoke in both possible positions; sometimes the rod hole is not exactly centered in the thickness of the part.

You can remove excessive clearance by taking a little material off the flat face of the guide block. If any binding is detected, increase the clearance of the crank handle in the yoke. When everything suits you, glue the guide block to the backplate, and the back to the baseplate. When the glue has dried, finish and wax all the components. (See Illus. 2-36.)

## Assembling the Mechanism

To assemble the mechanism, insert the crank assembly into the backplate and push in the axle pin. Illus. 2-51 and 2-52 show a tool you can make to do this more easily. Set the yoke on the crank handle and slide the guide rod down through its block and into the hole in the yoke, keeping the two pencil dots aligned. Line up the holes and push in the short pin. You have now completed another mechanism to add to your collection.

NO. 44 (.086) DIA
$\frac{5}{16}$ DEEP

$\frac{3}{16}$

ROD $\frac{5}{16}$ DIA X 6

$\frac{1}{64}$

AXLE PIN INSERTING TOOL

*Illus. 2-51.*

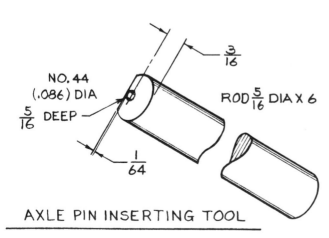

*Illus. 2-52. Using the assembly tool to insert the small pin in the Scotch Yoke axle.*

# FAST-RETURN ACTUATOR

*Illus. 2-53. The Fast-Return Actuator.*

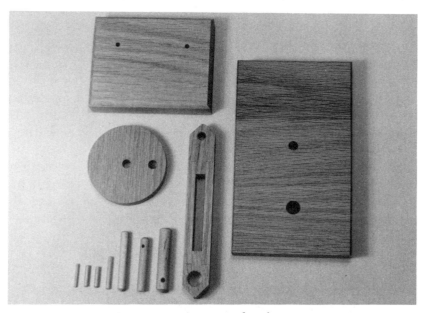

*Illus. 2-54. The parts for the Fast-Return Actuator.*

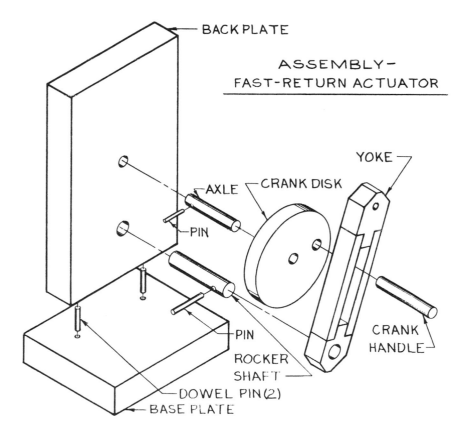

BACK PLATE

ASSEMBLY—
FAST-RETURN ACTUATOR

YOKE

AXLE

CRANK DISK

PIN

CRANK
HANDLE

PIN

ROCKER
SHAFT

DOWEL PIN (2)

BASE PLATE

*Illus. 2-55.*

The fourth model in the series is another version of a pin-and-slot mechanism. It is used in applications where a slow, powerful working stroke is desired in combination with a rapid return stroke. This action can be found in metal shapers and slotters, reciprocating power saws, and other machinery having similar requirements.

## Making the Parts (Illus. 2-56)

The backplate of this device has an axle-bearing hole identical to the one in the Scotch yoke previously described, only the locations differ. The same instructions apply for fitting

the axle, for making the crank disk, and for assembling these components, so I won't repeat them here, but will refer you to the preceding sections. The only new instructions for this unit will give details of the yoke and its pivot axle. (See Illus. 2-57.)

As the two end pieces of the yoke are very small, leave them attached to the larger block from which they are cut for as long as is possible. Plane a piece of material ²⁵⁄₃₂ inch thick, at least 1½ inches wide, and long enough to hold comfortably. Square one end of this piece and cut the central tenon across its width. If you flip the block to cut both sides at the same settings, the tenon should

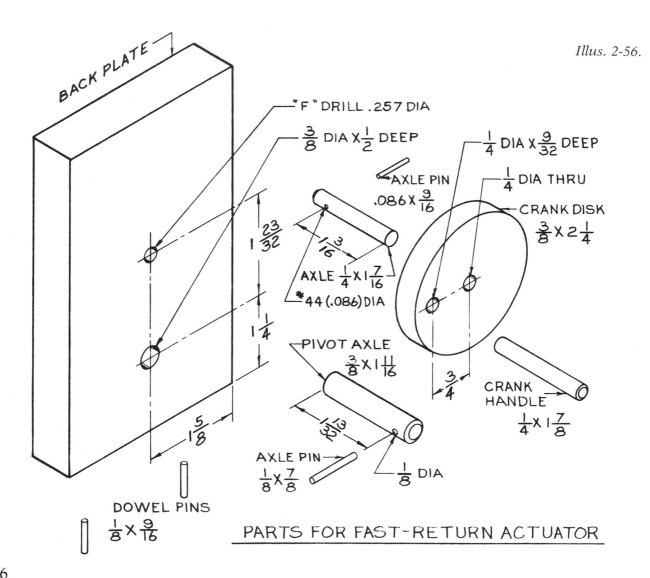

*Illus. 2-56.*

PARTS FOR FAST-RETURN ACTUATOR

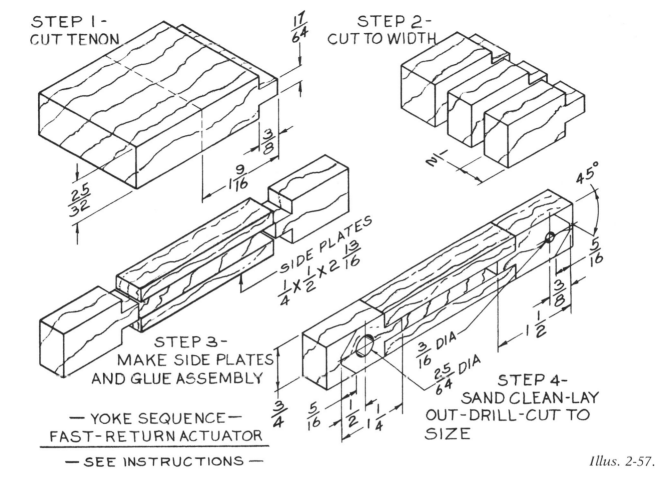

STEP 1 - CUT TENON

STEP 2 - CUT TO WIDTH

$\frac{17}{64}$

$\frac{3}{8}$

$\frac{9}{16}$

$\frac{25}{32}$

2

SIDE PLATES $\frac{1}{4} \times \frac{1}{2} \times 2\frac{13}{16}$

STEP 3 - MAKE SIDE PLATES AND GLUE ASSEMBLY

— YOKE SEQUENCE — FAST-RETURN ACTUATOR

— SEE INSTRUCTIONS —

45°

$\frac{5}{16}$

$\frac{3}{8}$

$1\frac{1}{2}$

$\frac{3}{16}$ DIA

$\frac{25}{64}$ DIA

$\frac{3}{4}$

$\frac{5}{16}$

$\frac{1}{2}$

$1\frac{1}{4}$

STEP 4 - SAND CLEAN-LAY OUT-DRILL-CUT TO SIZE

*Illus. 2-57.*

be accurately centered. Make several cuts to get to the $\frac{17}{64}$-inch dimension, as this dimension must not be cut undersize. If you have a problem at this stage, just saw off the tenon and try again.

When the dimensions are satisfactory, saw off the end so that it's a little over 1½ inches long. Rip this end into two ½-inch-wide pieces. (See Illus. 2-58.) As it is a lot easier to work on a large part, don't do the remaining work on these pieces until the yoke assembly has been glued.

Plane a couple of pieces to ¼ × ½ inch for the yoke side plates, and cut each to a length of exactly 2¹³⁄₁₆ inches. Make a pencil mark to identify the outer face of each piece, and finish the other, inner face of each to a smooth surface.

Make a trial assembly of the four parts to check for any unsightly gaps, and, if none exist, apply glue sparingly and assemble the yoke. Place squares of cardboard under a small clamp on each end, and pull the assembly up snug by applying a large clamp on the long axis of the part. Then tighten the small clamps and loosen the large one. (See Illus. 2-59.)

Remove any squeezed-out glue from inside the slot as explained in the section on the Scotch yoke. When the glue has dried, sand the part clean, lay out the holes and the corner angles, and drill and shape these details to complete the part. (See Illus. 2-60.)

In all but its length, the pivot axle is identical to the axles in the first two mechanisms. If you made the drill jig, place the stop pin in hole number 3 to drill this part. Sand the diameter of the pin so that it can be push-

*Illus. 2-58. The blank and two yoke end pieces.*

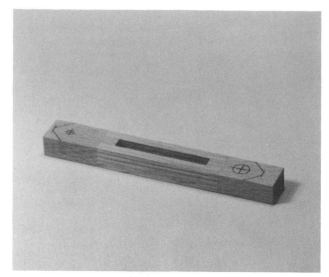

*Illus. 2-60. The yoke laid out so that it can be trimmed to its final shape.*

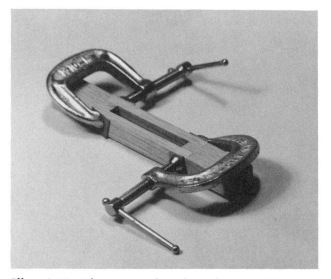

*Illus. 2-59. Gluing together the yoke assembly.*

fitted snugly into its hole in the backplate. Make the two axle pins and the two dowels for the back-to-base assembly.

## Assembling the Mechanism

You should by now have completed the crank disk assembly, which, as previously stated, is identical in all but a few dimensions to the one for the Scotch yoke. (See Illus. 2-61.) Proceeding with the assembly, insert the crank axle into its bearing hole in the back-

plate. Wipe a little glue around the inside of the pivot axle hole, and place the axle into the hole. Put the yoke in place, insert a long rod in the axle pin hole to help keep it level, and tap in the axle until the pin hole is about 1/32 inch from the yoke. Remove all loose parts and glue the back to the base. When it is dry, clean up the parts, apply a finish, and wax the moving surfaces. Assemble all the parts and push in the two axle pins. Try the mechanism. It is now complete and ready to display. (See Illus. 2-54.)

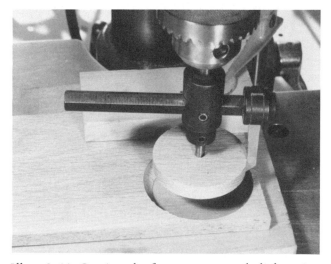

*Illus. 2-61. Cutting the fast-return crank disk, using the circle cutter with disk-cutting bit.*

48

# SELF-CONJUGATE CAM

*Illus. 2-62. The Self-Conjugate Cam.*

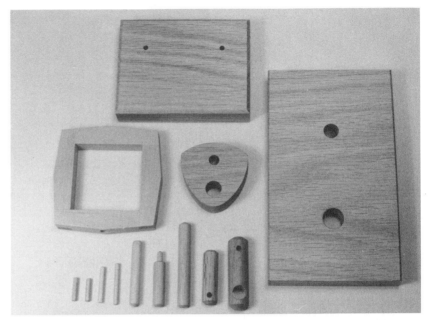

*Illus. 2-63. The parts for the Self-Conjugate Cam.*

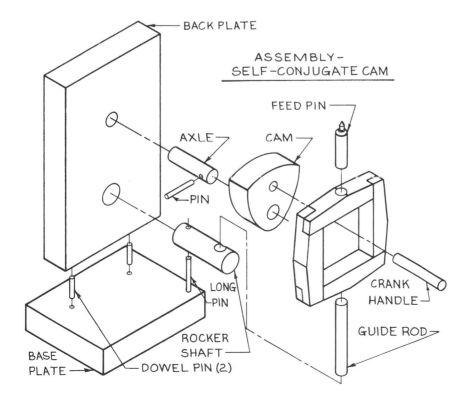

BACK PLATE

ASSEMBLY–
SELF–CONJUGATE CAM

FEED PIN

AXLE

CAM

PIN

LONG
PIN

ROCKER
SHAFT

DOWEL PIN (2)

BASE
PLATE

CRANK
HANDLE

GUIDE ROD

*Illus. 2-64.*

49

While the more common form of rotary cam requires an external force, such as a spring or gravity, to keep its follower in contact, the self-conjugate cam positively controls its follower, eliminating this dependence. A cam of this type can be operated in any desired position, and can rotate at high speed, with no possibility of "floating" of the follower that limits the speed of conventional designs.

This particular device is known as the Mitchell Motion, named for its inventor, and has been in use for many years for stepping film through motion-picture equipment. Its unusual action makes this an interesting display model.

## Making the Parts (Illus. 2-65)

In all but the hole layout, the backplate for this model is identical to the one for the eccentric, so review the instructions for that model. The cam axle and the rocker shaft are also exact duplicates of those on the eccentric. The only parts that are unique to this model are the cam and its follower yoke.

Make the yoke first, as it is much easier to fit the cam to it than the other way around. Plane a piece of straight-grained stock that's at least 3 inches wide to a thickness of ½ inch. Square one end, and cut off a piece 2 $\frac{29}{32}$ inches long.

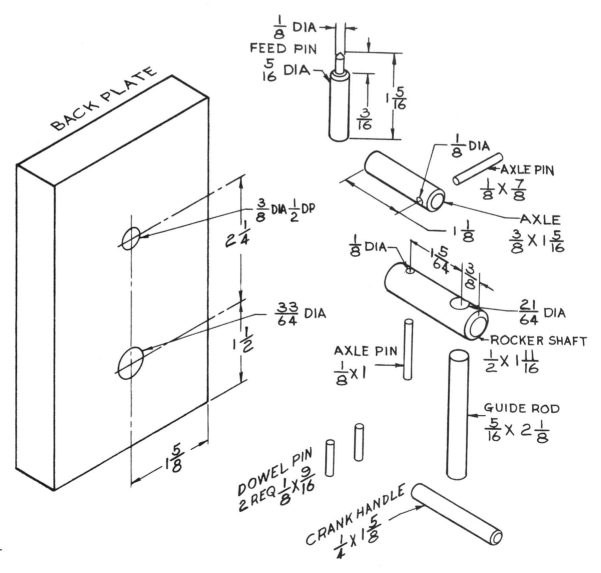

*Illus. 2-65.*

50

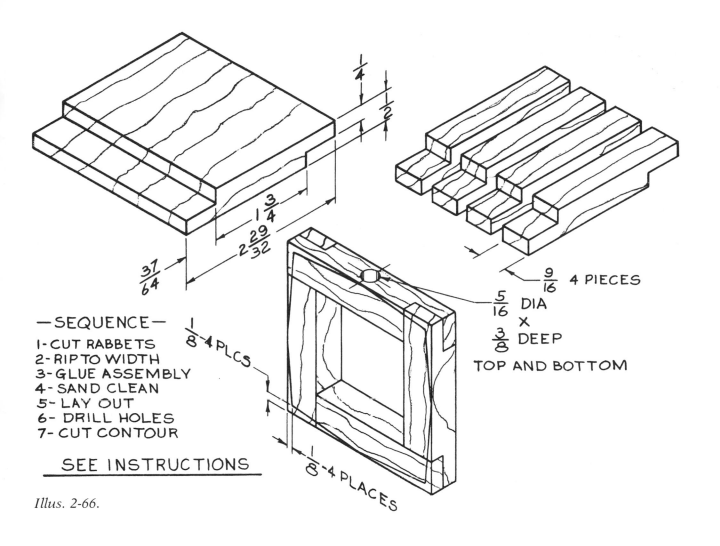

$\frac{1}{4}$

$\frac{1}{2}$

$1\frac{3}{4}$

$2\frac{29}{32}$

$\frac{37}{64}$

$\frac{9}{16}$ 4 PIECES

$\frac{5}{16}$ DIA

X

$\frac{3}{8}$ DEEP

TOP AND BOTTOM

—SEQUENCE—

1- CUT RABBETS
2- RIP TO WIDTH
3- GLUE ASSEMBLY
4- SAND CLEAN
5- LAY OUT
6- DRILL HOLES
7- CUT CONTOUR

SEE INSTRUCTIONS

$\frac{1}{8}$-4 PLCS

$\frac{1}{8}$-4 PLACES

*Illus. 2-66.*

Now, cut the corner half-lap joints across both ends of the piece as shown in Illus. 2-66 and 2-67, making the cuts as close as possible to one-half the thickness of the stock. A table-mounted router is a good tool for cutting the half-lap joints, if you have one. Note that the joints are cut ¹⁄₆₄ inch too long, which gives some extra material to trim after gluing. When the half-lap joints are cut, rip the piece into four widths, as shown in Illus. 2-68.

Temporarily assemble the yoke, and mark the outer face of each piece with a pencil. Don't omit this step, as it's very easy to assemble these parts backwards. Now, sand the inner face of each piece, and remove any fuzz or splintering from the joints. Apply glue sparingly and assemble the yoke, using one small clamp at each corner. (See Illus. 2-69.) Gently tighten these four clamps, apply a larger clamp alternately across the width and height to draw the joints snug, tighten the corner clamps, and allow the glue to dry, removing any excess from inside the yoke. When the glue is dry, flat-sand the two faces and trim the excess stock at the four corners.

Lay out and drill the two holes for the guide rod and the feed pin, taking care that the drill point doesn't break through to the inside of the yoke. All that remains is to lay out the angled contours on the four sides and

*Illus. 2-67. The yoke blank with half-lap joints cut on each end, on the router table.*

*Illus. 2-68. The four yoke sides cut from a blank.*

*Illus. 2-69. Gluing together the yoke assembly.*

cut and sand to the lines. Finish-sand the part, lightly rounding all corners.

Having completed the follower yoke, now make the cam. Glue a photocopy of the cam pattern shown in Illus. 2-70 onto a piece of ⅝-inch-thick stock. (See Illus. 2-71.) Be sure to lay a steel ruler across the graduations on the photocopy to check the reproduction's size. Many photocopiers make oversized prints, and that won't do for this application.

Drill the axle and handle holes, and saw the part to its outline with a band saw. Sand carefully to the line, and test the fit in the yoke. Allow at least ¼64-inch clearance at all points of rotation, and more if you are working in a very dry environment. I once made a

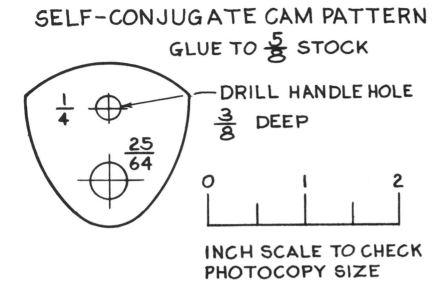

# SELF–CONJUGATE CAM PATTERN
## GLUE TO $\frac{5}{8}$ STOCK

*Illus. 2-70.*

—DRILL HANDLE HOLE
$\frac{3}{8}$ DEEP

$\frac{1}{4}$

$\frac{25}{64}$

0        1        2

INCH SCALE TO CHECK
PHOTOCOPY SIZE

*Illus. 2-71. The cam pattern glued to a blank.*

motor-driven display model that locked solid when the West-Coast-winter humidity took effect. The cam should measure exactly the same at any two diametrically opposed points around its contour when checked with a caliper. Hand-sand the contour in the direction of rotation, finishing with 240-grit or finer abrasive.

Cut the guide rod from a piece of ⁵⁄₁₆-inch dowel, and sand and fit it into one of the holes in the yoke. Glue the rod in place, checking its parallelism as explained in the instructions for the preceding designs.

Make the feed pin, and glue it into the remaining hole in the yoke. The small, turned end section is nonfunctional in this model, so you can leave it at its full diameter if you don't have a lathe.

The remaining parts are the handle, the two axle pins, and the two small dowel pins, all of which are identical to those in earlier designs. (See Illus. 2-63.) Glue the handle into the cam, and then glue the axle into the backplate, tapping it in until its pin hole is just clear of the cam. Review this procedure in the cam and follower instructions, if necessary.

Assemble the back to the baseplate, clean up the parts, and apply a finish. When the finish is dry, wax the bearing surfaces and assemble the model. The action of this mechanism will intrigue almost everyone.

If you made all five models, you now have an interesting and unique set of wooden mechanisms. Have fun with them.

# CHAPTER 3

# Stationary Steam Engine

This is a model of a type of engine that was in common use until the middle of the twentieth century. I saw large versions of this engine operating in 1946, and a few are still in daily service in the United States. Since a steam boiler can be designed to be heated by any locally available fuel, such engines are ideal for use in remote areas, where they can still be found. Because of its many visible moving parts, the steam engine remains a perpetual favorite, making this model a desirable project.

## HOW THE MECHANISM WORKS

A sliding valve above the steam cylinder is actuated by an eccentric on the crankshaft. This valve admits steam pressure at the end of each stroke, to the side of the cylinder that the piston is approaching, while simultaneously admitting the steam from the other side of the cylinder to the exhaust port. As both "in" and "out" strokes of the piston deliver power to the crankshaft, this is known as a "double-acting" engine.

*Illus. 3-1. The Stationary Steam Engine.*

55

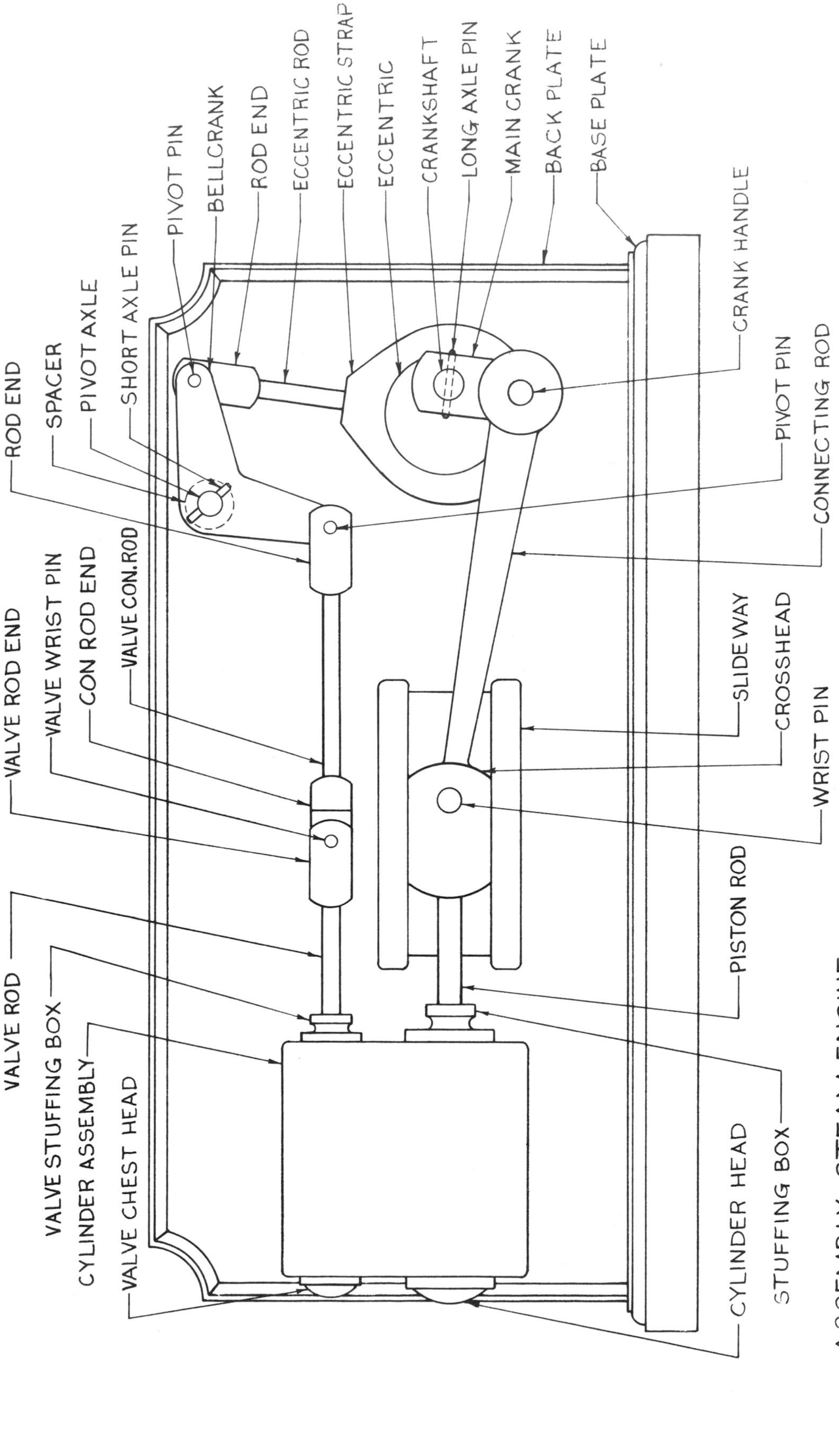

ASSEMBLY—STEAM ENGINE

PIVOT PIN
BELLCRANK
ROD END
ECCENTRIC ROD
ECCENTRIC STRAP
ECCENTRIC
CRANKSHAFT
LONG AXLE PIN
MAIN CRANK
BACK PLATE
BASE PLATE

ROD END
SPACER
PIVOT AXLE
SHORT AXLE PIN

CRANK HANDLE

PIVOT PIN
CONNECTING ROD

VALVE ROD END
VALVE WRIST PIN
CON ROD END
VALVE CON.ROD

SLIDE WAY
CROSSHEAD
WRIST PIN

VALVE ROD

VALVE STUFFING BOX
CYLINDER ASSEMBLY
VALVE CHEST HEAD

PISTON ROD

CYLINDER HEAD
STUFFING BOX

*Illus. 3-2.*

56

## BUILDING THE MECHANISM

You should have built some of the models in the preceding chapter before attempting this project. This model is not recommended for beginners. There are many small parts that must be properly made and fitted, so follow the instructions closely unless you are experienced with small work.

## DRILL JIG

As good alignment of the many components is essential for a smoothly operating engine, you should first make the drill jig shown in Illus. 3-4 and 3-5. This tool locates all holes in the backplate and its mating parts, including dowel holes for the back-to-base assembly.

Square up a piece of hardboard or plywood that is ⅛ to ¼ inch thick to the dimensions indicated in Illus. 3-5. Make a very careful layout; then check the dimensions again. If the dimensions are correct, drill the holes as shown. When you have made the jig, start on the actual components of the model.

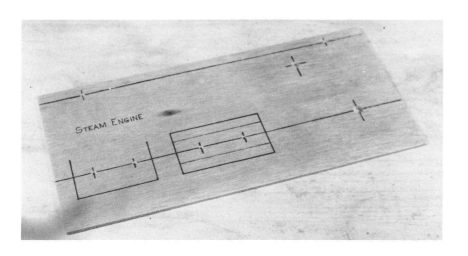

*Illus. 3-4. The drill jig.*

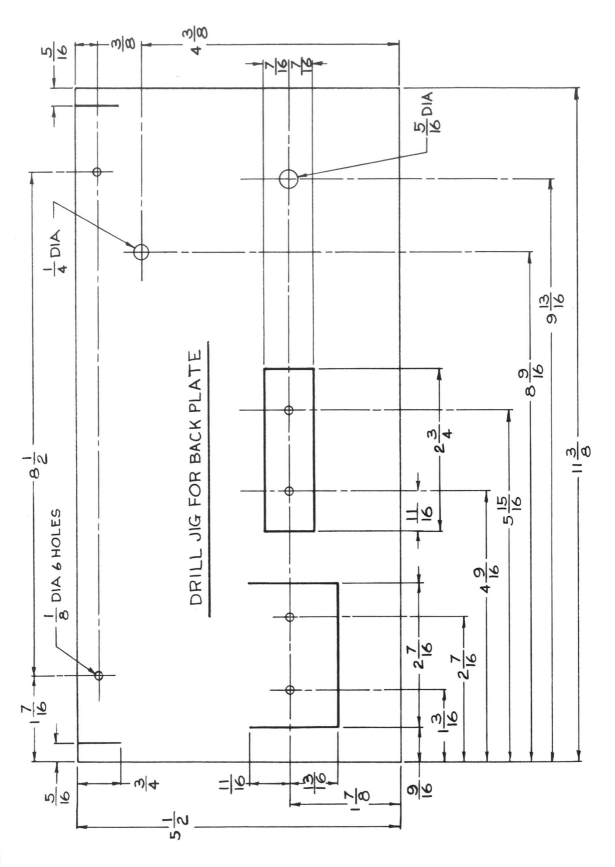

DRILL JIG FOR BACK PLATE

58

*Illus. 3-5.*

## MAKING THE PARTS

### Backplate and Baseplate (Illus. 3-6 and 3-7)

Select for these parts a neutral-colored wood that does not have a prominent grain pattern, to best show off the moving parts. Joint and plane the material to its proper thickness. Cut the baseplate to its finished size. Before doing the same thing to the backplate, decide if you want to make the coves on the upper corners and the quarter-round bead. These decorative cuts are not essential, so you can omit them if you do not have the equipment for this work. If you decide to omit them, cut the backplate to its finished size. If, however, you want to include them, do the following:

1. Cut the blank about ⅜ inch longer and ¼ inch wider than its final dimensions. Lay out the length, width, and the cove radii, dividing the extra material equally all around. (See Illus. 3-8.)

2. Make the cove cuts with a band saw, and sand the coves to the lines, using a small drum sander. You can finish-sand the cuts by using 240-grit garnet paper on a split dowel, running in the drill press.

3. With a steel square and a marking knife or other blade, score the cross-grained end lines deeply all around the block. This will help prevent splintering when you trim the block to its finished length. (See Illus. 3-9.)

4. Flat-sand the two faces of the part with 240-grit paper. It is generally considered good practice to do all cutting before any sanding, but as sanding after small mouldings are cut will often destroy the sharpness of detail, I make this compromise, and accept the possible wear on the cutter from embedded abrasive grains.

5. Set up a table-mounted router with a ⅛-inch-radius beading bit. Adjust the height of the cutter above the table so that the two shoulders of the bead are cut exactly equal. Make test cuts on scrap material, until you

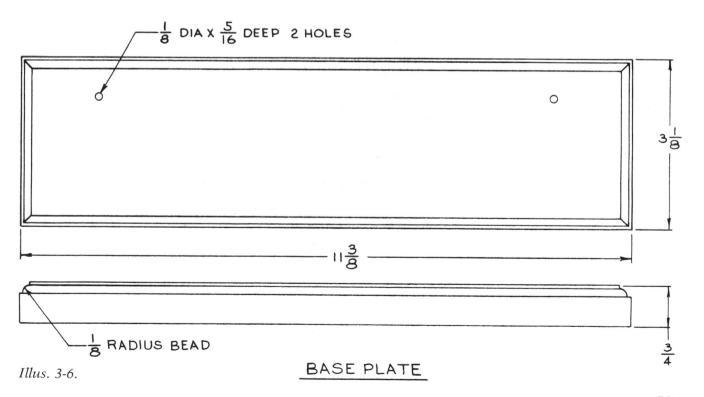

*Illus. 3-6.*

BASE PLATE

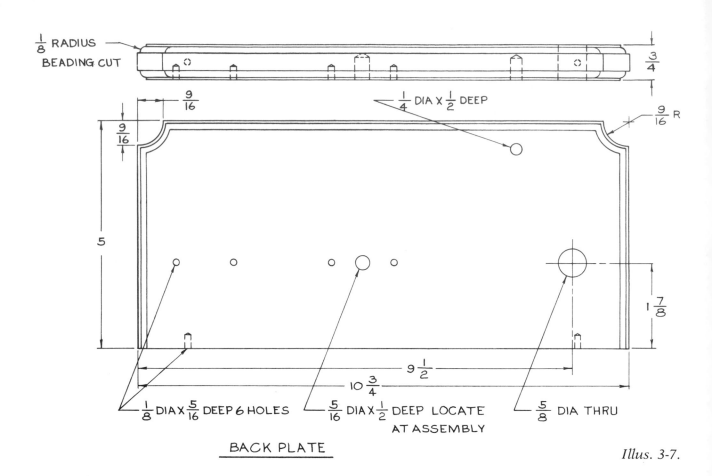

$\frac{1}{8}$ RADIUS BEADING CUT

$\frac{3}{4}$

$\frac{9}{16}$

$\frac{1}{4}$ DIA X $\frac{1}{2}$ DEEP

$\frac{9}{16}$ R

$\frac{9}{16}$

5

$1\frac{7}{8}$

$\frac{1}{8}$ DIA X $\frac{5}{16}$ DEEP 6 HOLES

$\frac{5}{16}$ DIA X $\frac{1}{2}$ DEEP LOCATE AT ASSEMBLY

$\frac{5}{8}$ DIA THRU

$9\frac{1}{2}$

$10\frac{3}{4}$

BACK PLATE

*Illus. 3-7.*

*Illus. 3-8. The backplate laid out.*

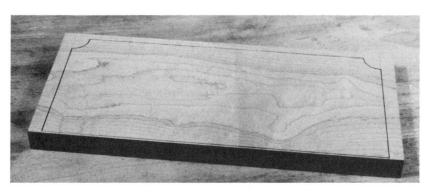

have this just right. I like to slow down the router by 30 to 40 percent; this allows me to feed the work slowly and maintain good control over it; this way, there is no chance that the wood will be scorched.

6. Cut the beads around both faces of each cove. As one of the cuts at each end of the part is fed into the grain, you will undoubtedly see some chipping at the entrances or exits of

these cuts. This is the reason for the extra material on the blank. Sand the beads very lightly if necessary, using only fine-grit sandpaper to remove fuzz. (See Illus. 3-10.)

7. Set up a sharp, clean-cutting blade, and saw the extra material off each end, cutting just outside of the knife lines. Sand the end surfaces clean and smooth with 240-grit abrasive.

60

*Illus. 3-10. A cove with beading.*

8. Saw the excess height off the top edge only, planing it smooth, and fine-sanding lightly if needed.

9. Cut the beads on the ends of the part. To avoid chipping at the cove cuts, start all the end cuts in the coves and feed out to the bottom edge. If you make one cut at each end with the part flat on its face, and one cut with the part vertical against a fence, proper direction of feed can be maintained. This is why the shoulders of the beading cut should be exactly equal. Illus. 3-11 shows this operation.

10. Cut the beads on the upper edge, and, last of all, trim the extra material from the lower edge. You should now have a finished part with crisp, uniform decorative beading all around.

Now, cut the beading all around the upper surface of the baseplate; use a small, square scrap block as a pusher to minimize chipping on the cross-grain cuts, which should be made first.

Lay out the center of the crankshaft bearing hole on the backplate. Drill a 5/8-inch hole at this location; clamp the part to a backup block to avoid chipping when you drill through. (See Illus. 3-12.) Select a piece of 5/8-inch hardwood dowel for the bearing and sand it to a close fit in the backplate hole. Cut the bearing to length, and chamfer its back end, leaving the front square.

Finish-sand the back face of the plate, raising the grain if necessary; it will be difficult to do this later. Glue the bearing in place, with its front end flush with the surface of the plate. Let it dry, and sand it clean. Carefully mark the center of the dowel, and draw a short vertical line through this point.

Place the drill jig on the plate, its lower edge flush with that of the part, and, looking into the hole in the jig, center the line drawn on the bearing face. Clamp the jig in place, drill all the holes to the depths shown, and remove the jig. (See Illus. 3-13.) Small errors may cause your crankshaft bearing hole to be something less than perfectly centered in the 5/8-inch dowel, but this will not affect

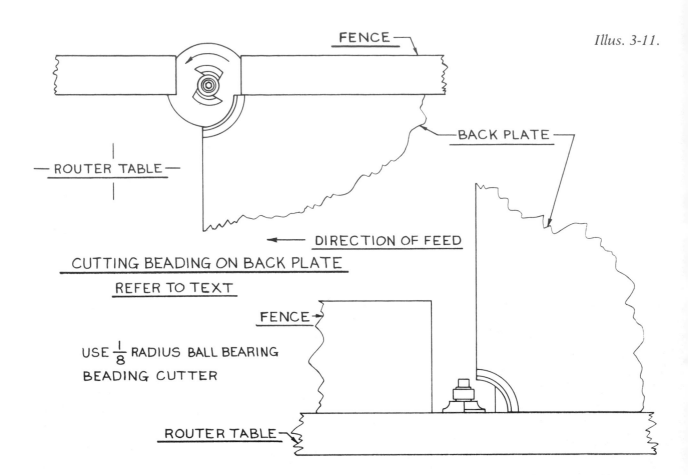

FENCE

*Illus. 3-11.*

BACK PLATE

ROUTER TABLE

← DIRECTION OF FEED

CUTTING BEADING ON BACK PLATE

REFER TO TEXT

FENCE →

USE $\frac{1}{8}$ RADIUS BALL BEARING
BEADING CUTTER

ROUTER TABLE

*Illus. 3-12. The backplate with the large hole for the bearing.*

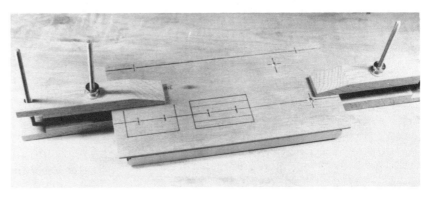

*Illus. 3-13. The drill jig clamped to the backplate.*

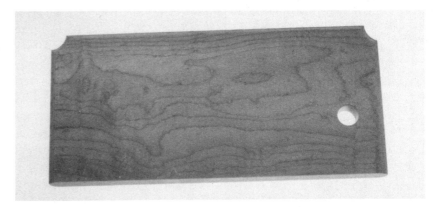

operation, and won't be noticeable after assembly.

Set the drill jig on two blocks to provide clamping clearance, and place the backplate upright on the jig. The rear face of the plate should be flush with the top edge of the jig, and the length of the backplate accurately centered over the two locating lines. (See Illus. 3-14.) Clamp the backplate securely, invert it, and drill the two dowel holes.

*Illus. 3-14. The backplate clamped to the jig for drilling dowel holes.*

The only work that needs to be done on the baseplate is drilling the dowel holes. Lay the jig on the plate with its edges ¼ inch in from the rear edge of the part. It does not have to be exactly ¼ inch in, as long as you keep the jig and the plate parallel to each other. Both ends of the jig should be flush with those of the part. If there is any difference in length, center the jig and the plate with each other. (See Illus. 3-15.) Clamp the jig and drill the two holes.

Clean up the parts and dry-assemble them with two dowels. Check for any large gaps at the joint, and correct these using a scraper or a small plane. When the fit is acceptable, assemble the parts; apply glue very sparingly, to minimize squeeze-out. Clamp the joint securely; check for squareness, and remove any excess glue after it has gummed up enough not to smear. Put the assembly aside to dry. You are ready for the next step.

## Cylinder and Valve Chest

This is a thick part that you may have to build from two or more pieces of wood. Keep any glue joints well away from the hole locations, and orient the grain direction as shown in Illus. 3-16. Glue the assembly and let it dry thoroughly before proceeding further. (See Illus. 3-17.)

Square-up the block and sand the end grain smooth enough to show the layout lines

*Illus. 3-15. The drill jig clamped to the baseplate.*

*Illus. 3-16.*

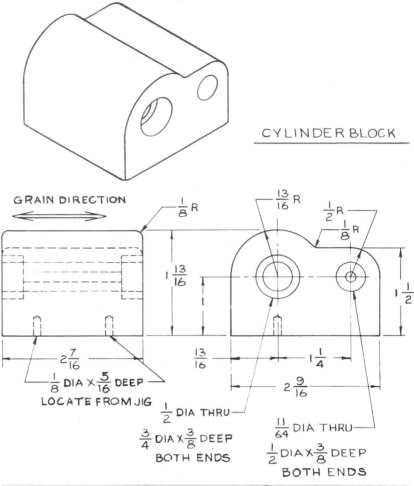

CYLINDER BLOCK

GRAIN DIRECTION

*Illus. 3-17.*

clearly. Lay out the hole centers on both ends, and draw the contours of the part, using a pencil compass. (See Illus. 3-18.) Using brad-point or spade drills, bore the shallow coun-

terbores in both ends of the cylinder and valve chest; then drill the central holes all the way through. (See Illus. 3-19.) The hole for the valve rod is shown undersized; it will be

64

*(Right) The Geneva Wheel has an intermittent output motion—the driven member is prevented from moving except when actually driven. (Below) The Loose-Link coupler is based on a very old design used in farm equipment It is loosely fitted and can operate in very dirty conditions.*

A

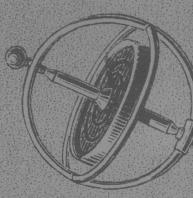

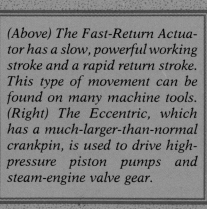

*(Above) The Fast-Return Actuator has a slow, powerful working stroke and a rapid return stroke. This type of movement can be found on many machine tools. (Right) The Eccentric, which has a much-larger-than-normal crankpin, is used to drive high-pressure piston pumps and steam-engine valve gear.*

B

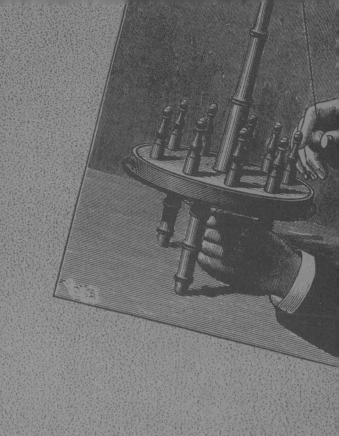

(Above) The Self-Conjugate Cam, which can operate at high speeds, has an unusual motion that makes it an interesting display model. (Right) The Scotch Yoke is a very compact substitute for the crankshaft-and-connecting rod used in most engines.

(Above) The Cam-and-Follower has a contoured rotary cam that gives a desired sequence of motions to its follower. (Right) The Intermittent Drive is a simple mechanism that will drive for half a revolution, pause for half a revolution, and then drive another half revolution.

D

*(Left) The Roller-Gearing model is a compact mechanism that requires less lubrication than other gears. (Below) The Stationary Steam Engine is modelled after a type of engine that was in use in the United States until the middle of the twentieth century.*

E

*The Positive-Action Cam provides absolute control of the position of its follower, under all conditions of operation. Top: a front view of the Positive Action Cam. Above: a rear view.*

F

*(Above) The shafts in the Double-Slider coupler have a ¼-inch offset, but still turn smoothly. (Below) The Universal Joint actually has two sets of universal joints that, when assembled, are known as a Constant-Velocity coupler.*

The Sun-and-Planet mechanism (above) was invented in 1775 by James Watt as a substitute for the more common crankshaft. (Right) The Single-Part Feed mechanism is a wooden version of a very common feeding system.

H

line-drilled to size through its stuffing box at assembly.

Cut the contour with a band saw and sand it; then round the corners as shown in Illus. 3-20. Now, set the cylinder block, with the valve chest towards the top, on the drill jig, and center it over its locating lines. (See Illus. 3-21.) Clamp it in place, invert it, and drill the two dowel holes $\frac{5}{16}$ inch deep. (See Illus. 3-22.) Sand the block smooth and clean, and put it aside to await assembly.

Illus. 3-20. Cutting out the cylinder contour on the band saw.

Illus. 3-18. The cylinder block laid out.

Illus. 3-21. The cylinder block clamped to the drill jig.

Illus. 3-19. Drilling the cylinder block.

Illus. 3-22. Drilling dowel holes in the cylinder block.

## Crosshead Slideway

The three parts of this subassembly can be cut to size on a table saw and sanded clean. (See Illus. 3-24.) Round the corners of the two outer members as shown in Illus. 3-23; also round the upper corners on the ends of the spacer block. Clamp the spacer block, accurately centered in its locating lines on the jig, and drill the two dowel holes ⅛ inch deep. (See Illus. 3-25.)

Using a marking knife and a steel square, scribe lines across the block at both edges of each dowel hole. Scribe these lines around the corner on one edge of the part; this will give you a set of marks on which to align your table-saw blade. Cut slots ¼ inch deep at each dowel hole location. (See Illus. 3-26.)

Leaving the saw setting undisturbed, put two short dowels into the crosshead slide location on the backplate and test the fit. The slots in the block should fit on the dowels

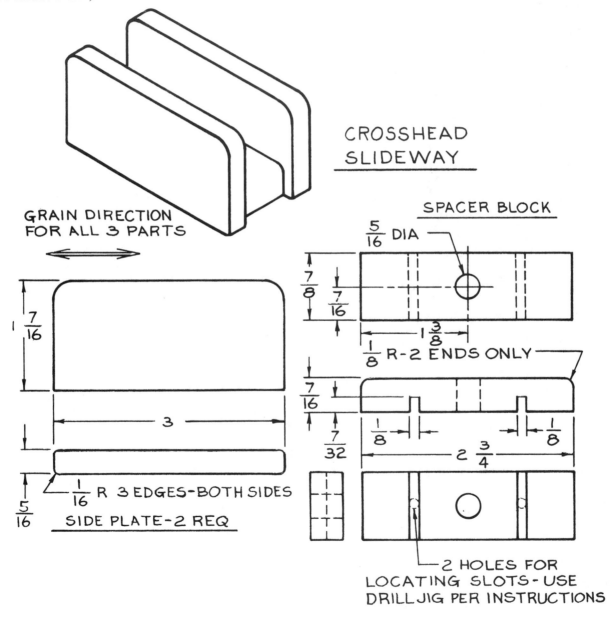

CROSSHEAD
SLIDEWAY

GRAIN DIRECTION
FOR ALL 3 PARTS

SPACER BLOCK

5/16 DIA

7/8    7/16

1 3/8

1/8 R-2 ENDS ONLY

7/16

7/32    1/8    2 3/4    1/8

1 7/16

3

1/16 R 3 EDGES-BOTH SIDES

5/16

SIDE PLATE-2 REQ

2 HOLES FOR
LOCATING SLOTS-USE
DRILL JIG PER INSTRUCTIONS

*Illus. 3-23.*

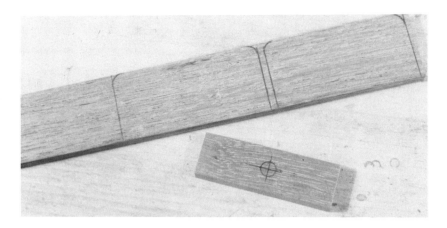

*Illus. 3-24. The parts for the slideway laid out.*

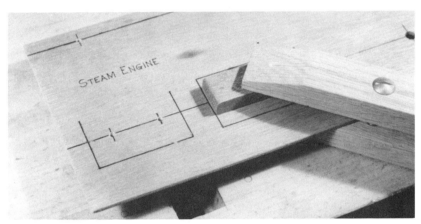

*Illus. 3-25. The slideway spacer block clamped to the drill jig.*

*Illus. 3-26. The slideway spacer block and the tools used to scribe and cut the slots in it.*

tightly, but still permit vertical adjustment. If the fit seems *too* tight, determine where stock needs to be removed, and trim a little in the appropriate slot. When this has been done, fine-sand all three parts and glue them together. Check that the sides of the clamped assembly are parallel to each other, to ensure that they don't lean in or out.

Once again, remove any excess glue from inside the assembly after it has become quite gummy, at which time it can be cleanly removed. When it is dry, flatten the base of the subassembly using a scraper or a small plane. This completes the crosshead slideway. (See Illus. 3-27 and 3-28.)

*Illus. 3-27. The completed slideway.*

*Illus. 3-28. The bottom of the completed slideway.*

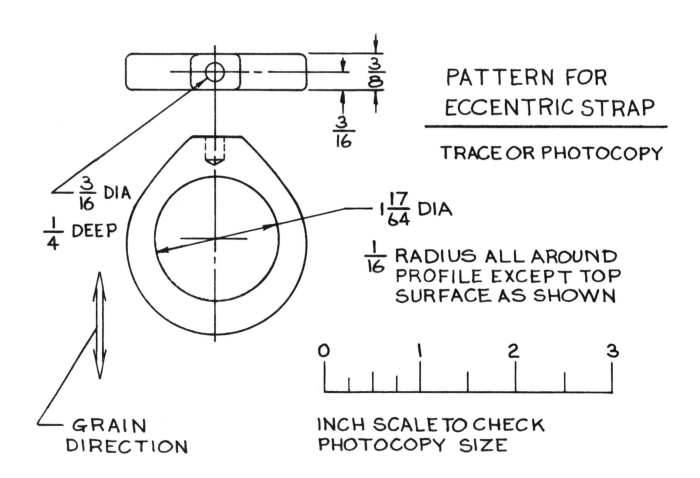

$\frac{3}{8}$

$\frac{3}{16}$

$\frac{3}{16}$ DIA

$\frac{1}{4}$ DEEP

$1\frac{17}{64}$ DIA

## PATTERN FOR ECCENTRIC STRAP

### TRACE OR PHOTOCOPY

$\frac{1}{16}$ RADIUS ALL AROUND PROFILE EXCEPT TOP SURFACE AS SHOWN

GRAIN DIRECTION

0    1    2    3

INCH SCALE TO CHECK PHOTOCOPY SIZE

*Illus. 3-29.*

## Eccentric Strap

Plane a piece of stock to slightly more than ⅜ inch to allow for sanding, and glue on a photocopy or a tracing of the eccentric strap. (See Illus. 3-29 and 3-30.) Using a small circle cutter, or whatever else you have, cut the center hole. (See Illus. 3-31.) If sanding is required to smooth the hole surface, do it now while you are working with a large piece of wood.

Cut the part with a band saw and sand it to size. Square the centerline across the end and mark and drill the rod hole. Grip the part in a drill vise with its centerline aligned with the jaws; this automatically puts the part square with the drill press table. (See Illus. 3-32.)

Round the corners, except for the flat upper edge, raise the grain, and finish-sand the part.

## Eccentric

Draw a circle for the eccentric and lay out and drill the 5/16-inch-crankshaft hole. (See Illus. 3-33) Cut out the circle with a band saw and sand it to size. Hand-sand in the direction of rotation. The part should have a minimum clearance in the eccentric strap of 1/64 inch, and up to 1/32 inch on the diameter if local humidity varies greatly. A vernier or dial caliper is a useful tool for getting similar parts round and accurately sized. (See Illus. 3-34.)

*Illus. 3-30. The eccentric strap pattern glued to the stock.*

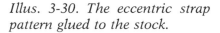

*Illus. 3-31. Cutting the center hole in the eccentric strap.*

*Illus. 3-32. Drilling the rod hole in the eccentric strap.*

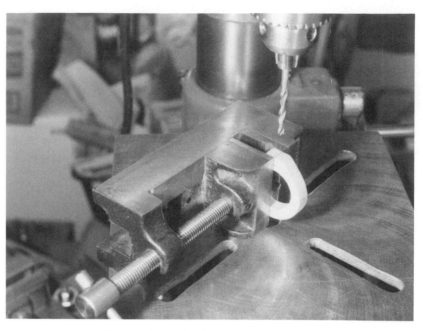

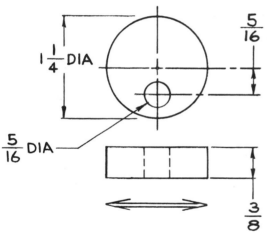

$1\frac{1}{4}$ DIA

$\frac{5}{16}$

$\frac{5}{16}$ DIA

$\frac{3}{8}$

*Illus. 3-33.*

*Illus. 3-34. The eccentric and the eccentric strap.*

## Connecting Rod

First, measure the photocopy of the pattern shown in Illus. 3-35 to make sure it is at its proper size; then glue it onto the stock. (See Illus. 3-36.) If the distance between the centers of the holes is noticeably longer than shown in Illus. 3-35, the piston rod may hit bottom at the end of its stroke. Drill the holes accurately, and saw out the contour. File and sand to the line; work carefully, as this is a highly visible part.

The undercut central web is not essential to the functioning of the model, but it does enhance its appearance. I cut away most of the excess material with a rotary planer, and complete the job with small chisels and files. (See Illus. 3-37 and 3-38.) Take your time and do a nice job on this. Round the corners on the central web only and fine-sand the entire part, just removing the sharp corners all around the two end bosses. (See Illus. 3-39.)

## Crosshead

Prepare a piece of material ¾ inch thick, and at least 2 inches wide by 5 inches long. (See Illus. 3-40.) Joint one edge smooth and square, lay out the part, and drill the wrist pin hole. (See Illus. 3-41.)

70

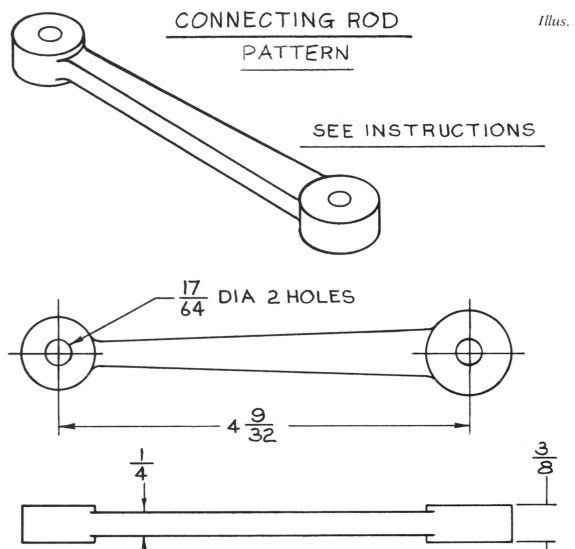

# CONNECTING ROD
## PATTERN

## SEE INSTRUCTIONS

$\frac{17}{64}$ DIA 2 HOLES

$4\frac{9}{32}$

$\frac{1}{4}$

$\frac{3}{8}$

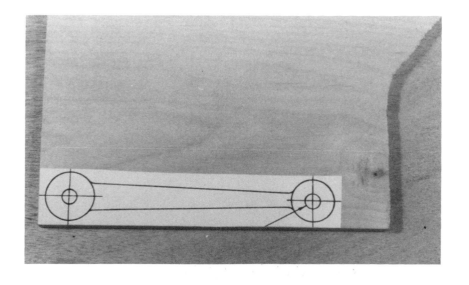

*Illus. 3-36. The connecting-rod pattern glued onto the stock.*

*Illus. 3-37. Cutting the web on the connecting rod.*

*Illus. 3-38. Rounding the end bosses.*

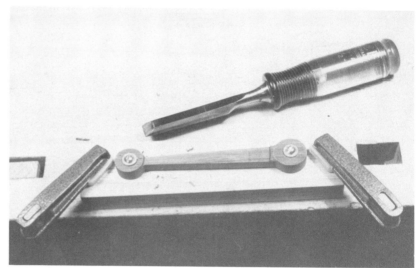

*Illus. 3-39. The completed connecting rod.*

# CROSSHEAD

$\frac{3}{8}$    $\frac{13}{16}$    $\frac{3}{8}$

$\frac{3}{8}$    $\frac{3}{4}$

$\frac{1}{4}$ DIA    $\frac{3}{8}$    $\frac{3}{16}$

$\frac{5}{8}$R

2 ENDS

$\frac{1}{4}$ DIA    1 $\frac{13}{32}$    $\frac{7}{8}$   $\frac{7}{16}$

*Illus. 3-40.*

*Illus. 3-41. The crosshead laid out.*

Set up a router table with a fence and insert a long ¼- or ⁵⁄₁₆-inch cutter. If your router table has a large center hole, clamp a thin wooden auxiliary table over it to support the small parts while cutting. Adjust the fence so that the cutter is centered reasonably well over the thickness of the part.

Use a square-edge pusher block to prevent chipping, and rout the slot to depth, taking cuts not more than ³⁄₃₂ inch deep. When the

depth is correct, move the fence a little at a time, flipping the part over to make a cut on both sides of the slot at each setting. (See Illus. 3-42.) The finished width of the slot should be a little over ⅜ inch. Cut the part to its finished outline, square the centerline across the solid end, and drill the rod hole parallel to all the faces of the part. Fine-sand all over, and lightly round all the sharp corners. (See Illus. 3-43.)

## Rod Ends

The procedures outlined below and shown in Illus. 3-46 keep these small parts attached to a large blank for as long as possible:

1. Plane a piece of stock so that it's ⅜ inch thick and about 2 inches wide by five inches long. The edges and ends should be square and parallel.

2. Mark two lines so that they are parallel to each edge; these lines represent the widths and centerlines of the parts. At one end of the blank lay out the valve-connecting rod end; its ³⁄₁₆-inch-thick tongue should extend outward. On both faces of the blank, cut with a knife the lines at the inboard end of the tongue. This will prevent splintering when you are cutting this detail.

At the other end of the blank, lay out the valve-rod end, with its slot facing outward. Lay out the remaining two rod ends in the middle of the block. A draftsman's circle template is a useful tool for drawing the end radii on these parts. (See Illus. 3-44.)

3. Using a sharp-pointed awl, accurately mark each hole location and drill the holes, paying careful attention to the diameters shown in Illus. 3-45.

4. The outer radius of the valve connecting-rod end should now be bandsawed and sanded to the line. The reason for doing this now is that the layout will be lost when the tongue is cut. (See Illus. 3-47.) To cut the tongue, you must have a table insert that comes right up to the saw blade. If you don't have one, cut one from wood, screw it in

*Illus. 3-42. Cutting the slot in the crosshead.*

*Illus. 3-43. The completed crosshead.*

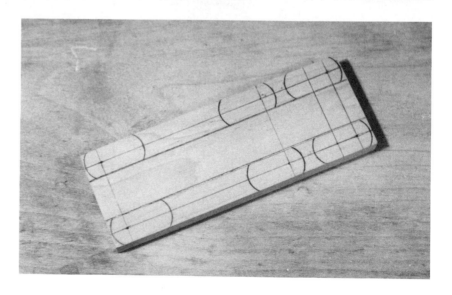

*Illus. 3-44. The layout for the rod ends.*

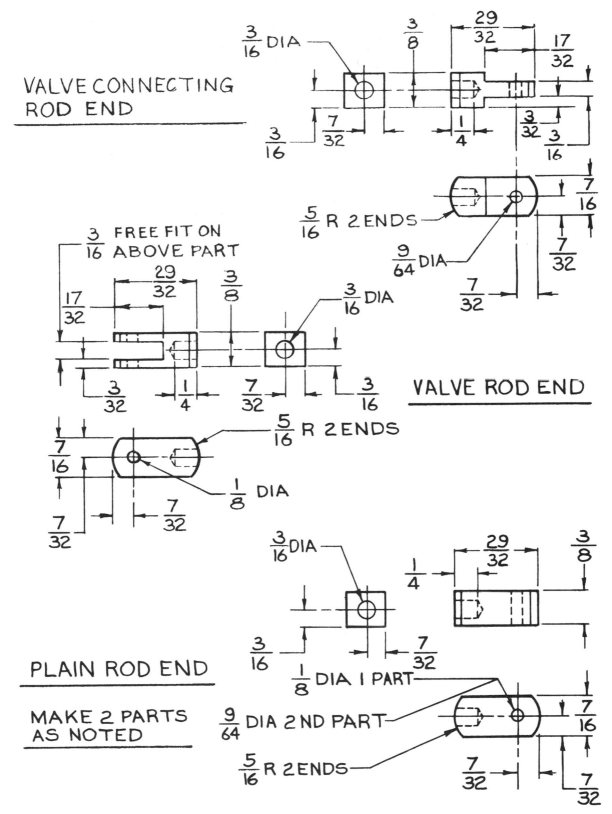

VALVE CONNECTING
ROD END

$\frac{3}{16}$ DIA

$\frac{3}{16}$

$\frac{7}{32}$

$\frac{3}{8}$

$\frac{1}{4}$

$\frac{29}{32}$

$\frac{17}{32}$

$\frac{3}{32}$

$\frac{3}{16}$

$\frac{5}{16}$ R 2 ENDS

$\frac{9}{64}$ DIA

$\frac{7}{32}$

$\frac{7}{16}$

$\frac{7}{32}$

$\frac{3}{16}$ FREE FIT ON
ABOVE PART

$\frac{17}{32}$

$\frac{29}{32}$

$\frac{3}{8}$

$\frac{3}{16}$ DIA

$\frac{3}{32}$

$\frac{1}{4}$

$\frac{7}{32}$

$\frac{3}{16}$

VALVE ROD END

$\frac{7}{16}$

$\frac{5}{16}$ R 2 ENDS

$\frac{1}{8}$ DIA

$\frac{7}{32}$

$\frac{7}{32}$

PLAIN ROD END

MAKE 2 PARTS
AS NOTED

$\frac{3}{16}$ DIA

$\frac{3}{16}$

$\frac{1}{8}$

$\frac{7}{32}$

$\frac{1}{4}$

$\frac{29}{32}$

$\frac{3}{8}$

$\frac{1}{8}$ DIA 1 PART

$\frac{9}{64}$ DIA 2 ND PART

$\frac{5}{16}$ R 2 ENDS

$\frac{7}{16}$

$\frac{7}{32}$

$\frac{7}{32}$

*Illus. 3-45.*

75

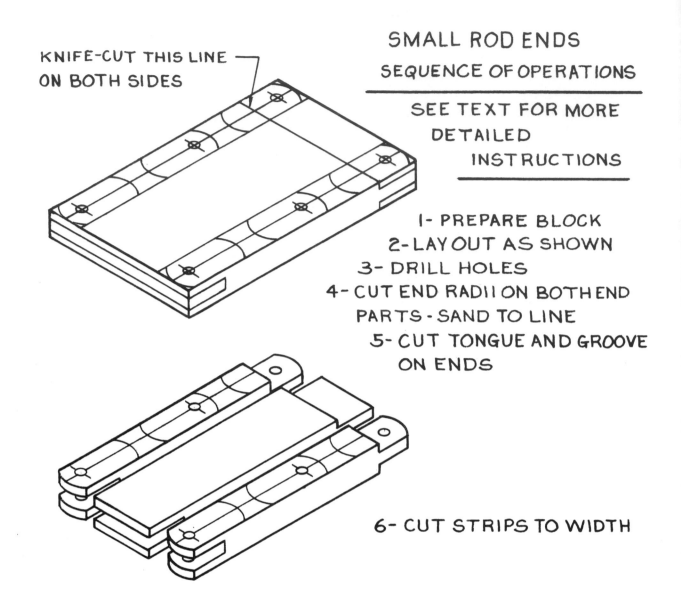

KNIFE-CUT THIS LINE
ON BOTH SIDES

# SMALL ROD ENDS
## SEQUENCE OF OPERATIONS

SEE TEXT FOR MORE
DETAILED
INSTRUCTIONS

1- PREPARE BLOCK
2- LAY OUT AS SHOWN
3- DRILL HOLES
4- CUT END RADII ON BOTH END
PARTS - SAND TO LINE
5- CUT TONGUE AND GROOVE
ON ENDS

6- CUT STRIPS TO WIDTH

7- CUT PARTS FROM STRIPS

8- LAY OUT AND DRILL ROD
HOLES IN ENDS

*Illus. 3-46.*

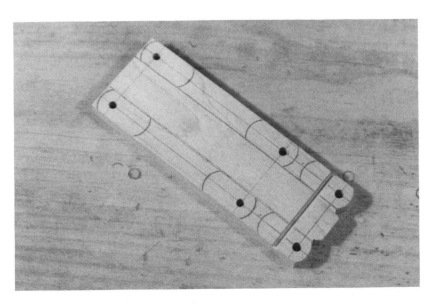

place, and feed the rotating blade up through it to saw its own slot. A close-fitting insert is an absolute requirement for safely working on small parts.

Set the blade to a height of ³/₃₂ inch above the table, and make the shoulder cut for the tongue on each face of the block. If you cut just short of the knifed lines, there should be no splintering. (See Illus. 3-48.)

Now, move the blade up to the full height of the tongue, and set the rip fence a little more than ⁹/₃₂ inch from the blade. Using a square piece of scrap for a pusher block, make a cut on each face of the part. Measure the thickness of the tongue and make very small adjustments to the fence until you get a thickness of ³/₁₆ inch. (See Illus. 3-49.)

Leaving the saw set at the same height, move the fence so that the saw blade is approximately centered over the thickness of the part. Invert the blank and cut the slot in the fork, using the same method as before to cut both sides equally. The slot should measure ³/₁₆ inch or slightly more. (See Illus. 3-50.)

5. Now rip the two pieces from the block, leaving just enough extra material for a plane shaving to remove saw marks. (See Illus 3-51.) Saw all the parts to their outlines and sand the end radii.

6. Lay out the centers of the rod holes in the ends of the parts. A small drill vise is a valuable accessory for drilling these holes. You can clamp the vise to your drill press table, using a stop piece to locate the work. When the position of these holes has been accurately centered under the spindle, all the rod holes can be accurately drilled. It's worth the trouble to make this setup. (See Illus. 3-52 and 3-53.)

7. Fine-sand the parts, and gently round the corners. (See Illus. 3-54.) Store these and other small pieces in closed jars or cans. If your shop is anything like mine, small parts that fall may never be seen again. I have occasionally seen parts that I thought were lost being crunched in the jaws of my Dalmatian.

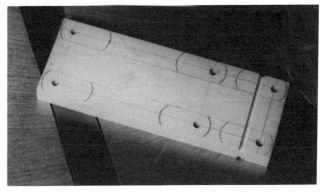

*Illus. 3-48. The first saw cut for the tongue.*

77

*Illus. 3-49. Cutting the tongue to its final thickness.*

*Illus. 3-50. Cutting the slot in the fork.*

*Illus. 3-51. The rod ends cut to their final width.*

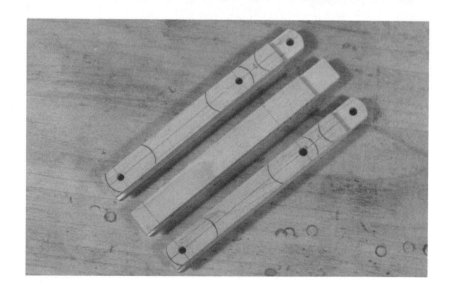

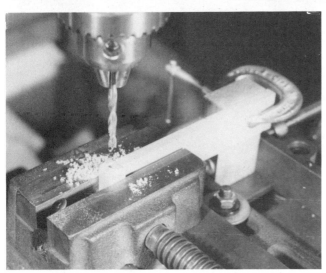

*Illus. 3-53. Drilling the rod holes.*

*Illus. 3-54. The completed rod ends.*

## Bellcrank

This part, shown in Illus. 3-55, and the main crank are cut from ⁷⁄₁₆-inch-thick stock, so it is advisable to plane material for both at the same time. Glue the bellcrank pattern to the wood, drill the holes, and cut out the outline with a band saw. (See Illus. 3-57.) Sand to the line, and round all corners. I use a ¹⁄₁₆-inch-radius cutter on the router table, and just run the part around on both faces. Fine-sand to the desired smoothness. (See Illus. 3-58.)

## Main Crank

Joint one edge of the stock and lay out the part as shown in Illus. 3-56. Drill the holes, cut out the part, and sand it to size. (See Illus. 3-59 and 3-60.)

## Remaining Parts

The remaining pieces, shown in Illus. 3-61 and 3-62, are made from dowel stock. A lathe is a definite asset for this work, but you can get by without one. Check the fits of the various parts in their respective holes, first determining which ones are running fits and which should be snug. Most of these pieces should be assembled by thumb-pressing them together. You definitely don't want any sledge-hammer fits on this small work. Note that it is a lot easier to sand a length of dowel to size before cutting it into little pieces.

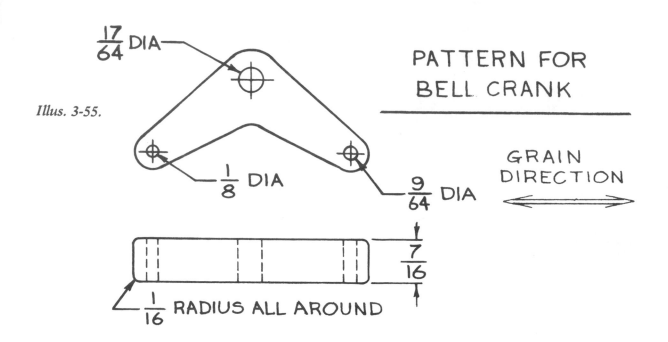

$\frac{17}{64}$ DIA

*Illus. 3-55.*

$\frac{1}{8}$ DIA

$\frac{9}{64}$ DIA

PATTERN FOR
BELL CRANK

GRAIN
DIRECTION
⟷

$\frac{7}{16}$

$\frac{1}{16}$ RADIUS ALL AROUND

## MAIN CRANK

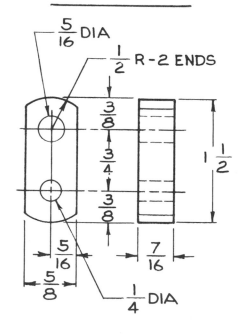

$\frac{5}{16}$ DIA

$\frac{1}{2}$ R-2 ENDS

$\frac{3}{8}$

$\frac{3}{4}$

$\frac{3}{8}$

$1\frac{1}{2}$

$\frac{5}{16}$

$\frac{5}{8}$

$\frac{7}{16}$

$\frac{1}{4}$ DIA

*Illus. 3-56.*

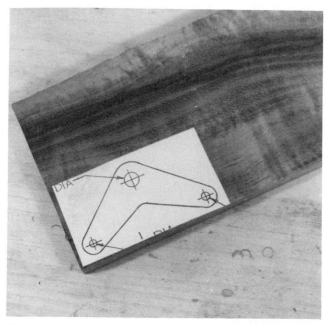

*Illus. 3-57. The bellcrank pattern glued onto the wood.*

*Illus. 3-58. The completed bellcrank.*

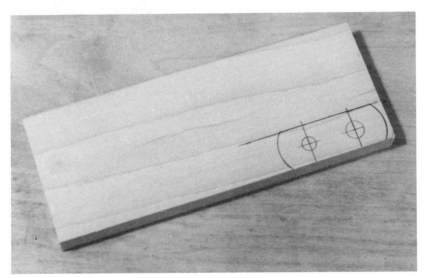

*Illus. 3-59. The main crank layout.*

*Illus. 3-60. The completed main crank.*

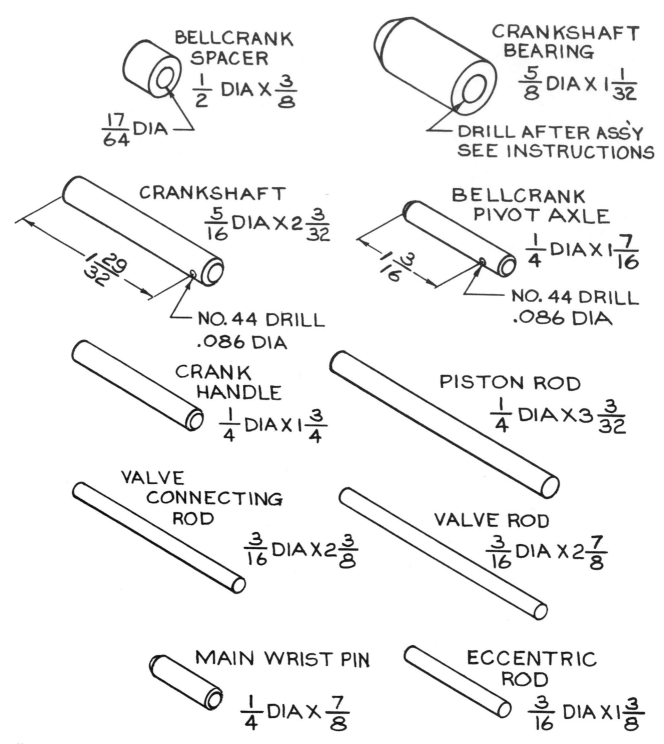

BELLCRANK SPACER $\frac{1}{2}$ DIA X $\frac{3}{8}$

$\frac{17}{64}$ DIA

CRANKSHAFT BEARING $\frac{5}{8}$ DIA X $1\frac{1}{32}$

DRILL AFTER ASS'Y SEE INSTRUCTIONS

CRANKSHAFT $\frac{5}{16}$ DIA X $2\frac{3}{32}$

$1\frac{29}{32}$

NO. 44 DRILL .086 DIA

BELLCRANK PIVOT AXLE $\frac{1}{4}$ DIA X $1\frac{7}{16}$

$1\frac{3}{16}$

NO. 44 DRILL .086 DIA

CRANK HANDLE $\frac{1}{4}$ DIA X $1\frac{3}{4}$

PISTON ROD $\frac{1}{4}$ DIA X $3\frac{3}{32}$

VALVE CONNECTING ROD $\frac{3}{16}$ DIA X $2\frac{3}{8}$

VALVE ROD $\frac{3}{16}$ DIA X $2\frac{7}{8}$

MAIN WRIST PIN $\frac{1}{4}$ DIA X $\frac{7}{8}$

ECCENTRIC ROD $\frac{3}{16}$ DIA X $1\frac{3}{8}$

*Illus. 3-61.*

## PIVOT PIN
**2 REQ**
$\frac{1}{8}$ DIA X $\frac{7}{8}$

## VALVE WRIST PIN
$\frac{1}{8}$ DIA X $\frac{9}{16}$

*Illus. 3-62. Remaining parts continued.*

## DOWEL PIN
**4 REQ**
$\frac{1}{8}$ DIA X $\frac{9}{16}$

## SLIDE WAY DOWEL
**2 REQ**
$\frac{1}{8}$ DIA X $\frac{7}{16}$

## AXLE PIN-LONG
.086 DIA X $\frac{11}{16}$

## AXLE PIN-SHORT
.086 DIA X $\frac{9}{16}$

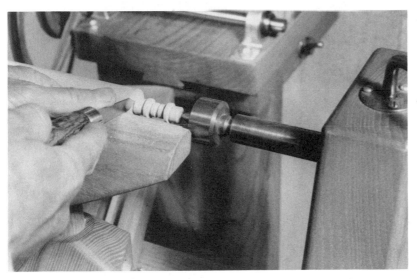

*Illus. 3-63. Turning the cylinder heads.*

Review the material in Chapter Two, if necessary, for details on making these parts.

Illus. 3-64 contains drawings for two different sets of cylinder heads and stuffing boxes. (Also see Illus. 3-63.) The simpler version is for those who don't own lathes. The end radii can be formed by twirling a dowel against a belt or disk sander. The stuffing boxes should have accurately-centered holes, so make these parts on the ends of lengths of dowel, and cut off any rejects, until you have things right. Fine-sand the parts, and glue the valve-rod stuffing box into place first. Let the glue set, and, using the hole in the stuffing box as a guide, drill a $\frac{13}{64}$-inch hole all the way through the valve chest. Now, clean out all chips and sawdust and glue in the remaining parts. This completes the assembly of the cylinder block. (See Illus. 3-65.)

# CYLINDER HEADS AND STUFFING BOXES

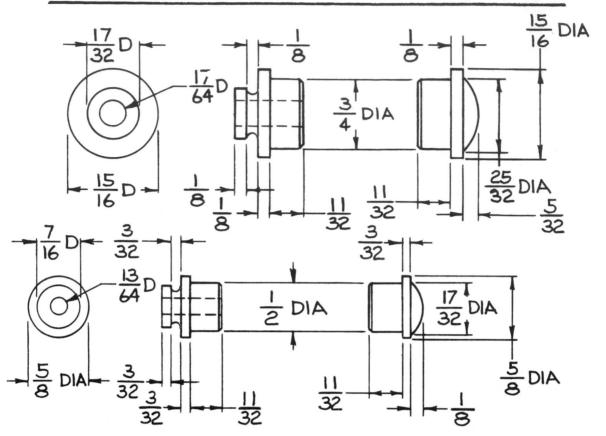

## ALTERNATIVE DESIGN

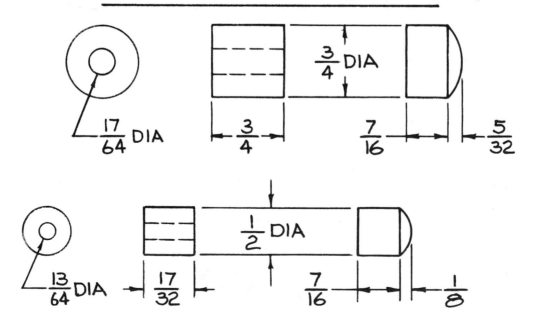

*Illus. 3-64.*

84

*Illus. 3-65. Assembling the cylinder heads and stuffing boxes to the cylinder block.*

# ASSEMBLING THE MECHANISM

## Crank

The parts shown in Illus. 3-2 are assembled for an engine with a clockwise rotation, but as this one doesn't run, it's not that important. Push the eccentric onto the crankshaft without glue; this is not a good assembly for gluing. Insert the crankshaft into its bearing on the backplate, and adjust the eccentric so that the small shaft-pin hole stands 1/64 inch clear of the back of the bearing.

Now, assemble the main crank, gluing it to the crankshaft and also to the eccentric. This will hold everything together. Remove any excess glue, and when the glue has dried sand the end of the shaft flush with the face of the crank. Glue the crank handle into its hole, checking it for squareness all around.

## Rod Ends and Eccentric Strap

On those rods that have parts at both ends, it is important to assemble everything in the same plane. Illus. 3-66 and 3-67 show a simple way to do this. Clamp the parts to a flat block, thus ensuring that their faces are aligned. Then check that all the edges are parallel in

*Illus. 3-66. Gluing the eccentric strap subassembly.*

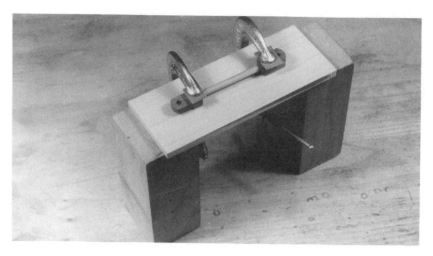

the vertical plane, using a straightedge. Needless to say, these parts must be gently clamped.

## Piston Rod and Crosshead

The piston rod must be parallel to all faces of the crosshead, or binding may result when the engine is operating. Hold each face in turn against a flat surface; any angular error of the rod will be readily visible. Check this several times, until the glue is firmly set.

## Pivot Pins

With the appropriate drawing in front of you, push the ⅛-inch pivot pins into their respective holes. No glue is necessary, unless the fits are too loose. Be careful; it's easy to put the pins in backwards at this stage.

Wipe a film of glue into the bellcrank pivot hole in the backplate. Put the pivot axle through the bellcrank and the spacer, and insert it into its hole. Tap it into the backplate until the little pin hole is about ¹⁄₆₄ inch from the face of the bellcrank. Remove all loose parts, and check the axle for squareness to the backplate.

The main and valve wrist pins and the two small axle pins are not glued in place, thereby permitting disassembly of the model when necessary. You should be able to push these pins in easily with your thumb.

## Cylinder Block and Crosshead Slideway

Unless you intend to use a very thin wipe-on finish, finish the components separately. Push two dowel pins into the backplate and set the cylinder block on them. Lightly clamp it with a padded clamp, and check that it fits flat all around. Take a sharp scriber or an awl and score a line all around the cylinder block, outlining its position.

It is essential that the crosshead slide is assembled correctly. One way to ensure this is to make and use the assembly tool shown in Illus. 3-68. Just saw a little block to the dimensions shown and you will have an adjustable parallel block that's ready for use. (You won't need the graduated scale shown on mine.)

Put the two short dowel pins in place and position the slideway on them. Set your adjustable parallel on the baseplate and adjust it so that the slideway looks about right. Now, insert the piston rod into its stuffing box and adjust the slideway up or down until the crosshead will slide freely with uniform clearance on top and bottom. Make certain that the slideway is sitting flat on the adjustable parallel, and then make a pencil mark across both parts of the parallel, for future alignment. Remove the crosshead and clamp the slideway in place. Scribe around it as for the cylinder block.

## ADJUSTABLE PARALLEL FOR ASSEMBLING SLIDEWAY SEE TEXT

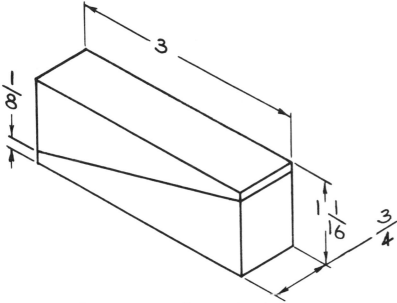

3

$\frac{1}{8}$

$1\frac{1}{16}$

$\frac{3}{4}$

*Illus. 3-68.*

Cut masking tape to fit inside the two gluing areas, keeping it about ¹⁄₁₆ inch from the scribed lines. Press the tape down quite firmly with a small wood block. (See Illus. 3-69.) Now, apply whatever finish you desire, sanding or rubbing with steel wool between coats. Don't saturate the tape with heavy, wet coats of finish, or you may dissolve the adhesive. Finish the cylinder assembly and the crosshead slideway, keeping the gluing areas as clean as possible.

When you are satisfied with the finish on the subassemblies, scrape their gluing surfaces. Remove the tape from the backplate, and scrape the areas where the two parts will be glued. I make small scrapers for this work, using old utility-knife blades set in handles and ground to shape. Scrape the surfaces almost, but not quite, to the scribed lines. Take your time with this operation, or you might have to repair your finishing job.

Put two dowel pins in the cylinder location,

*Illus. 3-69. The taped backplate, ready for a finish.*

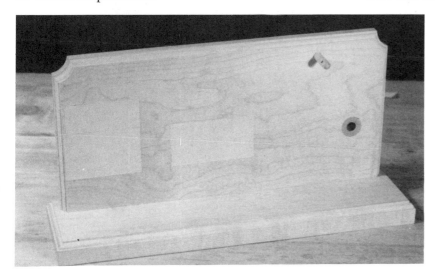

87

*Illus. 3-70. Gluing the cylinder and slideway to the backplate.*

set the cylinder in place, clamp it lightly, and check that it sits flat all around. If it looks all right, apply a thin film of glue to the cylinder block, keeping it at least ⅛ inch from all edges, and clamp it in position.

Repeat the above operation for the slideway, locating it with the adjustable parallel block as before. Clamp the assembly and remove any squeezed-out glue with a wet cloth, as water won't soak into your finished wood. Put the assembly aside to dry. (See Illus. 3-70.)

When you have removed the clamps, there is one more operation that you must perform. Drill through the hole in the slideway spacer and into the backplate ⁷⁄₁₆ inch deep, as shown in Illus. 3-23. (See also Illus. 3-71.) This is absolutely necessary so that the wrist pin has somewhere to go whenever you want to take the model apart.

Apply a finish to all the remaining parts. Use light coats of a thin finish, as these small parts can't tolerate a heavy buildup. Rub the parts to a uniform surface with steel wool. When the finish is dry, run drills through any bearing or pin holes that may have become partially filled. Remember that the two little axle pins should be no tighter than a mod-

erate push fit, and all bearings must move freely.

Wax all the moving parts; you can wax the whole assembly, if you wish. All the subassemblies are now complete. (See Illus. 3-2.)

*Illus. 3-71. Drilling the wrist-pin clearance hole.*

# FINAL ASSEMBLY

If you observe the following procedures, you will be able to assemble almost everything on the workbench, instead of on the model itself.

Assemble the valve train consisting of the valve rod, the valve connecting rod, the wrist pin, the bellcrank, and the eccentric strap. Place the bellcrank and its spacer onto the pivot axle on the backplate, and push in the short axle pin to retain the assembly. Work the linkage so that you can insert the valve rod into its hole in the valve chest. (See Illus. 3-72.) Operate this much of the assembly for a few strokes to ensure that all the parts move freely. Then swing the eccentric strap down over the crankshaft bearing hole, insert the crankshaft into its bearing, and slide the eccentric into its strap. (See Illus. 3-73.) Turn the crank a few times and, if all works correctly, push in the long axle pin on the back side of the crankshaft.

Slide, insert, or assemble the piston rod into the cylinder. The crosshead will probably fit better one way than the other, so make certain that it moves freely in its guides. Push the crosshead as far left as it will go, turn the crank handle all the way to the right,

*Illus. 3-72. Final assembly: Step one.*

*Illus. 3-73. Final assembly: Step two.*

and place the large end of the connecting rod on the crank handle. (See Illus. 3-74.) Turn the crank to the left, and slide the crosshead over the small end of the rod, until the holes line up. Push in the wrist pin. The model is complete.

If you ever need to disassemble the model, center the wrist pin over the hole in the middle of the slideway. Push the wrist pin out of the crosshead; the parts can now be removed in the reverse order of assembly. Now you have something unique to put on the mantel.

*Illus. 3-74. Final assembly: Step three.*

# CHAPTER 4
# Single-Part Feed Mechanism

In automatic-assembly equipment, a part often has to be delivered to a work station at exactly the right time so that it can be assembled with its mating components. The feed mechanism must, therefore, be synchronized with the other machinery.

This model is a wooden version of a very common feeding system which was also sometimes used in early mechanical coin-operated vending machines. The device adapts well to other equipment. People have built models from the photograph that appears in my magazine article (*American Woodworker*, September/October, 1989) and incorporated them in other marble mechanisms.

I have redesigned my original model for home workshop construction. The one described and shown here has a few more pieces, but you don't need three-dimensional routing capability to make it. You must, however, work closely to the drawing dimensions if you want a smoothly functioning model.

*Illus. 4-1. The Single-Part Feed mechanism.*

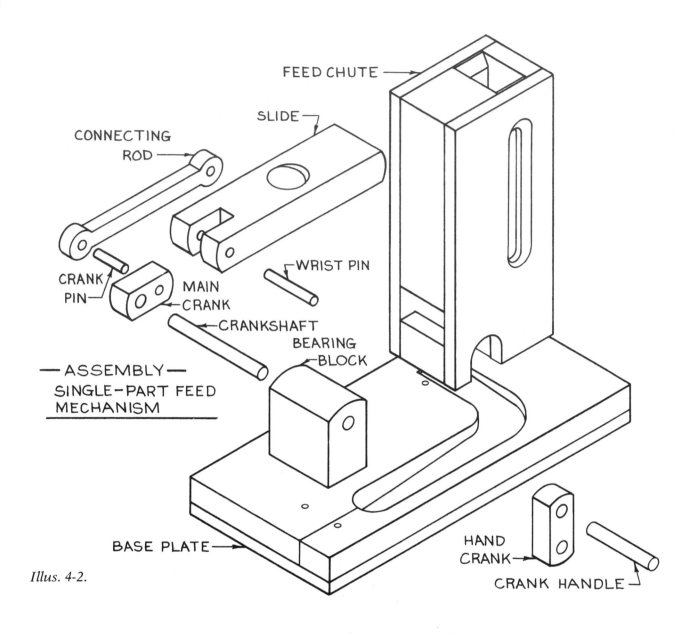

FEED CHUTE

SLIDE

CONNECTING
ROD

WRIST PIN

CRANK
PIN

MAIN
CRANK

CRANKSHAFT

BEARING
BLOCK

—ASSEMBLY—
SINGLE-PART FEED
MECHANISM

BASE PLATE

HAND
CRANK

CRANK HANDLE

*Illus. 4-2.*

## MAKING THE PARTS

## HOW THE MECHANISM WORKS

The workpieces, in this case marbles, are stacked in a supply chute. Rotation of the crank reciprocates a slide, shifting one part at a time to the delivery chute, where it drops into a storage track.

### Drill Jig to Locate Dowel Holes

Make the jig from a piece of hardboard or hardwood plywood. Location of the parts is critical, and would be difficult to do satisfactorily without a jig. Mark heavy lines for the part locations, and drill the holes as shown in Illus. 4-4.

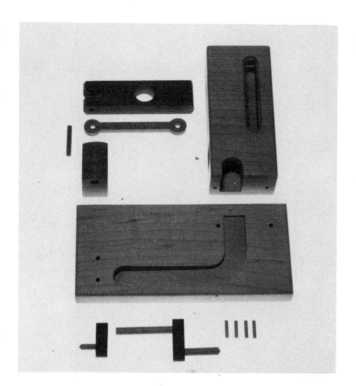

*Illus. 4-3. All the parts for the Single-Part Feed mechanism.*

DRILL JIG

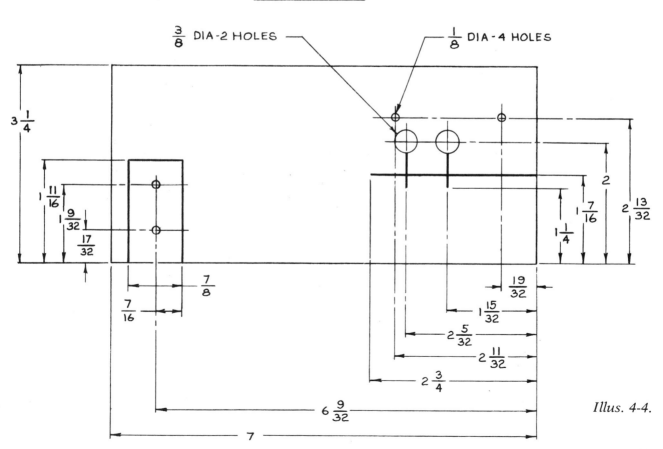

$\frac{3}{8}$ DIA-2 HOLES

$\frac{1}{8}$ DIA-4 HOLES

$3\frac{1}{4}$

$1\frac{11}{16}$

$1\frac{9}{32}$

$\frac{17}{32}$

$\frac{7}{8}$

$\frac{7}{16}$

2

$1\frac{7}{16}$

$1\frac{1}{4}$

$2\frac{13}{32}$

$\frac{19}{32}$

$1\frac{15}{32}$

$2\frac{5}{32}$

$2\frac{11}{32}$

$2\frac{3}{4}$

$6\frac{9}{32}$

7

*Illus. 4-4.*

93

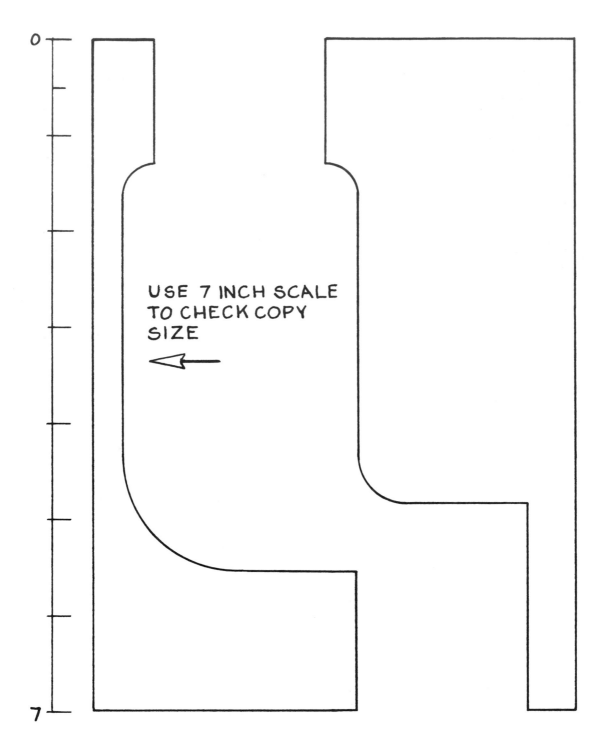

USE 7 INCH SCALE
TO CHECK COPY
SIZE

0
7

PATTERN FOR BASE PLATE – UPPER
MEMBER – GLUE TO $\frac{1}{2}$ INCH STOCK

*Illus. 4-5.*

## Baseplate Subassembly

Plane the material so that you have two thicknesses of ¼ and ½ inch. For a superior job, saw the bottom plate off a thick block, plane the minimum amount necessary to remove saw marks, and align the grain when gluing the assembly.

Photocopy or trace the upper base-plate member patterns in Illus. 4-5. If you have photocopied the patterns, check their sizes by comparing the seven-inch gradations on the left with those of a steel scale. Many self-service copiers are adjusted to give copies that are 102% of the original size. Most large-copy businesses have at least one machine that has infinitely variable magnification, and that will make copies at 100% of the original size.

Glue on the first half of the pattern. (See Illus. 4-6.) If you follow the sequence shown in Illus. 4-6–4-8, the end grain on the base-plate pieces will match, and you will get the most economic use out of the material. Cut the part out with a band saw and finish-sand it to the line. I use small drum sanders in the curves, and files and scrapers for the rest of the contour.

Glue on the second half of the pattern, and repeat the previous operations. (See Illus. 4-7.) Check the fits of the surfaces to be glued; if they are suitable, scrape the surfaces lightly and glue the two parts. When the glue has dried, flatten the bottom with a small plane and scrapers. If you use a small drum sander carefully, you will be able to blend in any small mismatch of the end-track radius. (See Illus. 4-8.)

*Illus. 4-6. The first half of the pattern glued to the wood.*

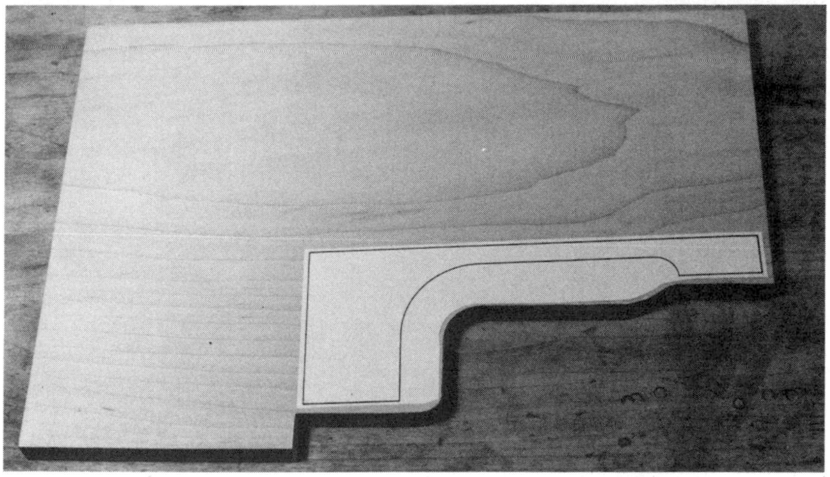

*Illus. 4-7. The second half of the pattern glued onto the wood.*

## Track Insert

Clamp the upper member to a piece of the same stock, and trace the track outline. (See Illus. 4-9.) I use a very sharp, hard lead in a draftsman's lead holder for this. Cut out the part with a band saw and finish-sand it to the line, using a belt sander on the outside contours, and a drum sander on the inside curves. The part should fit snugly, but not tightly, into the track. (See Illus. 4-10.)

Cut the piece for the bottom member so that it is at least ⅛ inch longer and wider than specified. Center the upper member on

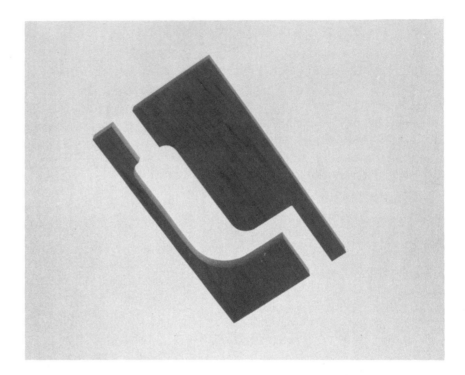

*Illus. 4-8. The completed parts of the upper baseplate member.*

*Illus. 4-9. Tracing the track insert.*

*Illus. 4-10. The track insert and the upper member.*

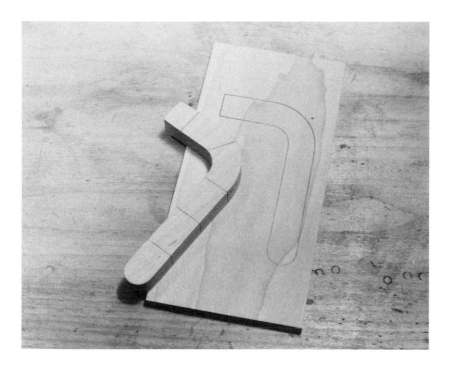

*Illus. 4-11. The insert and the baseplate with the traced outline.*

the part, and trace the track outline, to show the location of the insert. (See Illus. 4-11.) Lay out the slope of the insert as shown in Illus. 4-12, but don't cut it yet; this operation is a lot easier when the part is glued to the lower member. Scrape the bottom of the insert clean, apply a thin, narrow bead of glue, and set the insert in place in the pencilled outline. Use several small clamps, and

check that the part doesn't move while you are clamping it. (See Illus. 4-13.)

Allow the part to dry overnight, and then clamp it to the workbench, using the lowest profile clamps you can find. Carefully cut the slope of the insert, keeping its narrow width parallel to the base all around the part. I remove most of the stock with a chisel, and finish trimming to the line with a round-

97

*Illus. 4-12.*

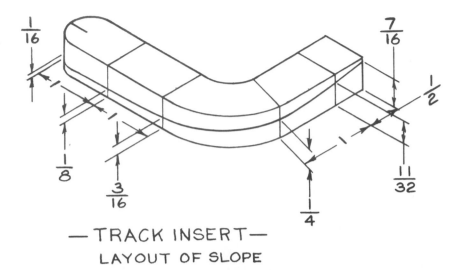

—TRACK INSERT—
LAYOUT OF SLOPE

*Illus. 4-13. The insert glued to the baseplate.*

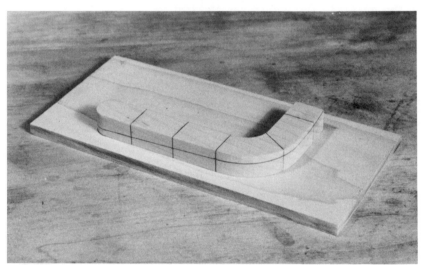

*Illus. 4-14. You can remove most of the stock with a chisel and trim to the line with a spoke-shave.*

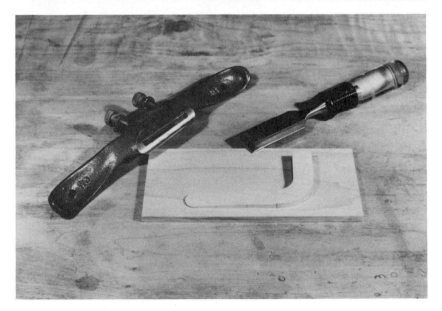

bottom spokeshave, but you could use a file and sandpaper. (See Illus. 4-14.) Try to achieve a smooth sloping surface, without bumps or hollows. If the wood needs to have its grain raised, do it now, as the surface of the track is unworkable after assembly.

## Completing the Base

Set the upper member in place, and check its fit with the lower member. If a gentle warpage has occurred on the thin plate, clamp the parts lightly before checking the fit. Make any indicated corrections, apply a film of glue to both surfaces, keeping the glue

well clear of the track and the insert, and clamp the parts. It's best to use a thick caul block on the bottom to help produce a flat assembly.

Unless you are in a hurry, give the assembly two days to dry before removing the clamps. If you do, the assembly will have a better chance of remaining flat. Now trim the part to size and round or chamfer the upper edges. (See Illus. 4-15.)

Align the lower edge of the drill jig with that of the baseplate. Look through the two ⅜-inch holes, and line up the edges of the track with the short vertical lines on the jig. (See Illus. 4-16.) Clamp the jig in place, and

*Illus. 4-15. The finished base.*

*Illus. 4-16. The drill jig clamped to the base.*

drill the four dowel holes. This completes the baseplate.

## Feed Chute Subassembly (Illus. 4-17 and 4-18)

The feed chute subassembly will look best if all its parts are cut from one thick block. If this is not practical, at least try to match the grain. Plane to the two thicknesses, and cut the front and back plates and the four core blocks, observing the grain direction indicated in Illus. 4-17.

Set up a fence on the router table so that the centerline of the viewing slot is in line with the spindle of the router. Clamp two end stops to control the length and position of the slot, and set up a $\frac{1}{4}$ inch router bit. Cut the slot in several passes, feeding the bit up to a maximum of $\frac{1}{16}$ inch at a time.

*Illus. 4-17.*

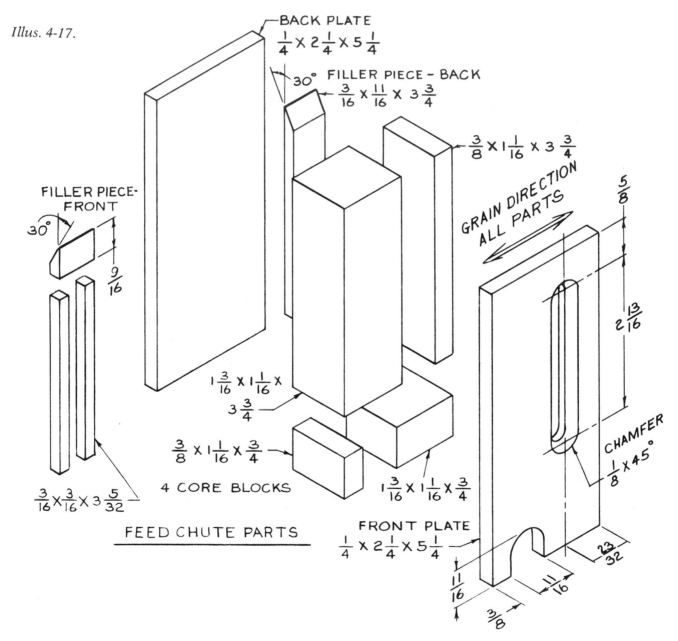

FEED CHUTE PARTS

*Illus. 4-18. The parts for the feed-chute subassembly.*

*Illus. 4-19. Cut the viewing slot with a router.*

Hold one end of the part firmly against both an end block and the fence, and lower the other end slowly onto the spinning bit. Feed the piece along to the other end stop, and lift the end off the bit. Work safely; keep your fingers well away from the area of the cut, and control the part at all times.

When you have cut through the thickness, substitute a ⁵⁄₁₆-inch bit for the first one, and cut the slot to size. Don't forget to check the positions of the two stop blocks, to avoid making the slot too long. (See Illus. 4-19.) I slow my router down so that it operates at about 40% of its top speed. This allows me to make cuts like this without having to worry about burning the wood. When the slot is cut to size, set up a 45° chamfering bit, if you own one, and cut the ⅛ inch × 45° chamfer.

Lay out the ball-exit cut on the plate, and make the cut with a band saw. Finish-sand to the line with a small sanding drum. Work very carefully, as the narrow piece on the side has a short-grain section, and can be easily broken.

Make the front and rear chute inserts by cutting them from a thick piece of stock. With the block upright against the table saw rip fence, and the fence adjusted ³⁄₁₆ inch from the blade, make cuts ¾ inch deep in the end grain on both sides of the piece. Then crosscut an ¹¹⁄₁₆-inch-wide piece from each face. Repeat the operation to cut the two narrow pieces. Making the cuts this way results in much straighter parts than cutting them from thin stock. Complete the parts as shown in Illus. 4-17. The narrow front inserts are very

101

*Illus. 4-20. The core blocks in place with the spacers inserted.*

fragile, but they don't take any stress, and they ensure that the grain directions will match properly. (See Illus. 4-18.)

Now, cut and plane a piece of stock from which to make the slide. Make this at least twice as long as the part. After you have finish-sanded the stock to its proper width and thickness, cut two blanks the length of the slide. You will use these two pieces as gluing spacers for the feed chute, thus establishing the correct fit for the completed slide.

Finish-sand the inner edges of the four core blocks. Set the front plate, with its inner face up, on a pair of blocks that will give you clamping clearance. Cut a couple of pieces of waxed paper and wrap them around three sides of each of the two pieces of stock you cut for the slide. Wipe glue on the tall, narrow core block, and clamp it in place, flush with the top and the edge of the front plate. Now, put one of the waxed-paper-wrapped blocks against this piece and glue the tall, wide core block to the plate, pushing it against the waxed-paper-wrapped spacer block.

Set the other half of the slide stock against the lower ends of the core blocks, and check that both blocks are in line. When they are

lined up properly, clamp the wide core block in place. Now, glue on the lower core blocks, keeping them snug against the slide piece, and clear of the ball exit gate. Put the parts aside to dry. (See Illus. 4-20.)

Remove the clamps and the paper-wrapped spacer blocks, and do any necessary clean-up work. Put just a little glue on the short, upper piece of the front insert, and position it flush with the top surface of the assembly. Clamp it in place for approximately 15 minutes, to give the glue a chance to set.

Put the two narrow insert pieces in position on both sides of the viewing slot, using a very small amount of glue. Now, remove the clamp from the upper piece, and set the spacer block you used originally on top of the three insert parts. Clamp it lightly and look in the viewing slot to make sure that none of the pieces has shifted. Tighten the clamp and allow the assembly to dry. (See Illus. 4-21.)

Check the flatness of the assembly thus far. Make sure that the backplate fits well and does not have any gaps. Glue on the backplate, checking the chute openings for squeeze-out, and remove any glue before it hardens.

102

Wipe a film of glue on the back insert, and slide it into place. Cut a narrow caul block to go into the chute, and another piece that will go through the viewing slot. This will allow you to clamp the spacer, as shown in Illus. 4-22.

Sand the entire assembly and round or chamfer all the corners, except around the bottom. Place the part upright on the drill jig, with its front surface on the line, and align both sides of the ball-exit slot with the two short, vertical lines. Clamp it in place, invert it, and drill the two dowel holes ⁵⁄₁₆ inch deep. (See Illus. 4-24.)

## Bearing Block

This part requires 1½-inch-thick stock, but can be glued up of two thicknesses. Be sure to observe the grain direction shown in Illus. 4-23. Square up the block, and lay out the hole center on each end. Draw the radius using a pencil compass or a draftsman's circle template. Drill undersize holes halfway through from both ends, and then finish drilling the holes with a full-sized drill, all the way through from one end. Saw and sand the radius.

Center the block over the two vertical lines

*Illus. 4-22. Clamping the rear insert using a caul block and a spacer.*

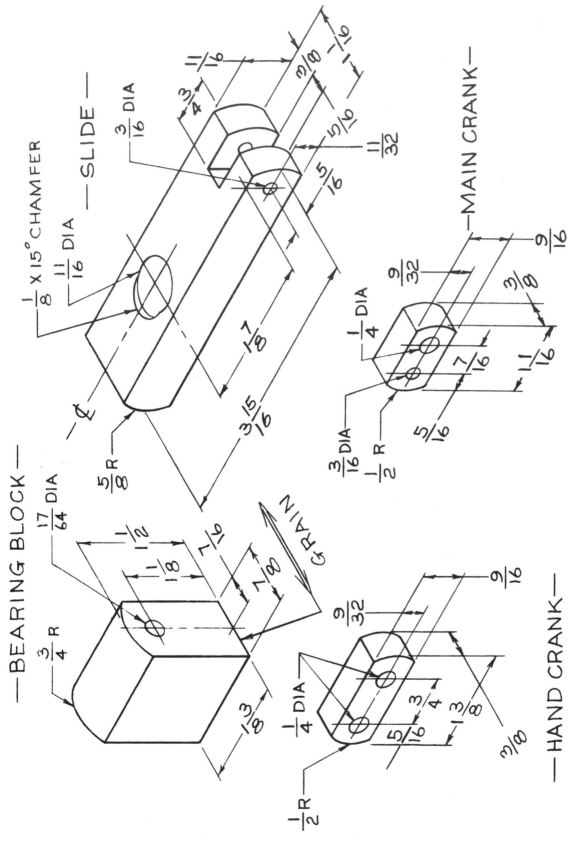

Illus. 4-23.

104

*Illus. 4-25. The bearing block clamped to the jig.*

on the jig, placing the upper end on the horizontal line. Clamp the block in place, and drill the dowel holes 5/16 inch deep. (See Illus. 4-25.)

## Slide (Illus. 4-23)

Make this part from one of the pieces that you used as spacers. Lay out the hole centers on both sides, and draw the end radii. Drill from both sides to the center, before cutting the slot. Slotting is best done on the table saw; make several cuts to remove the material. Illus. 4-26 shows a right-angle jig that I use on the saw. It backs up the workpiece to help prevent splintering, and also permits the clamping of small pieces that would be unsafe to hold by hand.

*Illus. 4-26. Cutting the slot in the slide.*

Drill the $1\frac{1}{16}$-inch-diameter hole, and cut the partial chamfer as shown in Illus. 4-23, using a gouge or a sharp knife. The chamfer dimensions are not critical, but this feature will make the action smoother on the backstroke.

Lightly chamfer the four long corners, to provide clearance in the slot, and test the fit of the slide in the feed chute. It should move easily, without excessive shake. Fine-sand the part, raising the grain if your material requires this.

## Connecting Rod

Plane the stock to the correct thickness, and glue on the photocopy of the pattern shown in Illus. 4-27; make sure that you have a full-size

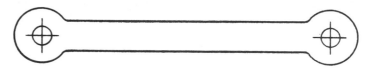

PATTERN FOR CONNECTING ROD

GLUE TO $\frac{1}{4}$ INCH STOCK

INCH SCALE –CHECK PHOTOCOPY

*Illus. 4-27.*

106

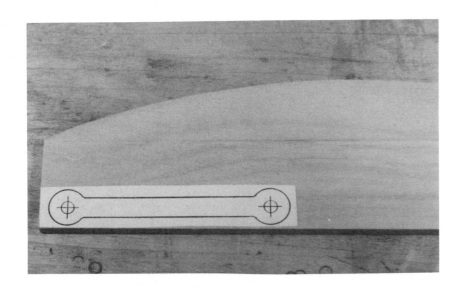

CRANKSHAFT

$\frac{1}{4}$ DIA X 2 $\frac{5}{32}$

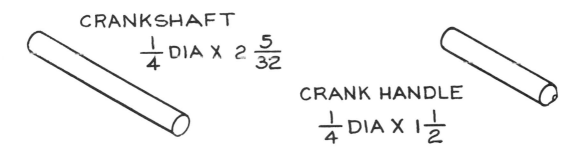

CRANK HANDLE

$\frac{1}{4}$ DIA X 1 $\frac{1}{2}$

CRANKPIN

$\frac{3}{16}$ DIA X $\frac{7}{8}$

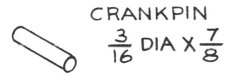

WRIST PIN

$\frac{3}{16}$ DIA X 1 $\frac{1}{4}$

DOWEL PIN - 4 REQ

$\frac{1}{8}$ DIA X $\frac{9}{16}$

photocopy, and not the normal oversize print. (See Illus. 4-28.) Drill the holes, and saw and file or sand the outline. Remove the pattern, and finish-sand the part.

## Crankshaft Assembly (Illus. 4-29)

There are five pieces to this component, and they should be fitted together in the sequence outlined below. The parts are similar to those for the steam engine in Chapter 3, so I won't repeat the instructions here.

Cut the crankshaft so that it's slightly oversize, and check that it fits and works well in the bearing block. Glue the shaft into the hand crank, sanding the end flush when dry. Glue the crank handle into the hand crank and sand it flush with the back side of the piece. Glue the crankpin into the main crank and sand it flush.

Now, insert the crankshaft into its hole in the bearing block. In a piece of cardboard about $1/64$ inch thick, cut a slot that will just clear the diameter of the crankshaft. Place this cardboard on the back face of the bearing block, around the crankshaft, and push the main crank onto the shaft until it is against the cardboard.

Now, place a marking knife or a chisel flat against the face of the main crank, with the cutting edge against the end of the shaft. Revolve the shaft a few turns to score a deep line around its circumference. Remove the main crank and cut off the end of the shaft, up to, but not past the line. Sand the end smooth, and lightly chamfer the sharp corner.

## Remaining Parts

The remaining parts are the wrist pin and the four dowels. Fit the wrist pin so that you can push it into its hole in the slide with your thumbs. (See Illus. 4-3.)

# ASSEMBLING THE MECHANISM

Make a trial assembly of all the parts, before gluing any of them. Set the feed chute and the bearing block in place, positioning them with the four dowels. Check that the dowels are not so long that they prevent proper assembly.

Put the crankshaft into its bearing, and push the main crank onto the inner end. Set the connecting rod on the wristpin. Now, insert the slide from the right side of the feed chute, pushing it to the left until the hole in the connecting rod is aligned with that of the slide, allowing you to push in the wristpin.

Drop a few marbles into the feed chute, and try the action. Turn the crank handle to reciprocate the slide. If the main crank is too free on the shaft, just turn it by holding the crankpin. The slide should pick up a marble at the right extremity of its stroke, and allow it to drop into the track when all the way to the left.

There is an extra $1/32$ inch of travel designed into both ends of the stroke, to absorb small cumulative errors, so your model should work fine. If you have any trouble due to errors in the dimensions of the pieces, you may have to elongate the $11/16$-inch hole on whichever end is necessary.

One word of caution is necessary: this device is designed to use standard $5/8$-inch-diameter marbles. While marbles slightly smaller or larger can be used, marbles much too large or too small will not work. The slide will not be able to move. One way to gauge the size of the marbles for this project is to drop them through the holes in a draftsman's circle template; reject those that are more than $1/16$-inch undersize or $1/32$-inch oversize.

When all the pieces have been assembled properly, glue the two parts to the base. Don't use too much clamping force on the feed chute, or you may collapse the $1/4$-inch walls. When the glue has dried, apply a finish to the parts. Soft pipe cleaners are handy for getting finish into narrow recesses.

Plug the hole in the main crank with a close-fitting dowel; use the dowel for a handle when applying a finish to the crank.

Tape the end ⅜ inch of the crankshaft to keep the finish off the gluing surface, and complete the finishing operations. Wax the parts when they have dried; work some wax into the bearing hole. Wax the crankshaft before removing the tape.

Now, insert the crankshaft into the bearing, remove the dowel from the main crank, and wipe a thin film of glue into the hole. Push the crank onto the shaft, so that the shaft is flush with the surface of the crank. Wipe away any excess glue with a damp cloth. The cranks look best when positioned 90° from each other, but it doesn't matter much.

Select seven nice marbles, and you are ready to display your handiwork. Children are fond of this device, so see to it that you have lots of extra marbles on hand.

# CHAPTER 5
# Couplings

The three models in this chapter demonstrate couplings used to join shafts that must be able to rotate together in spite of a certain amount of misalignment of their centerlines.

The first, and best known of these couplings is the universal joint. This unit is properly known as Hooke's Joint, after the 17th century inventor. While people are generally aware that these couplings are in their automobiles, not everyone knows what they look like. The mechanism in this chapter nicely displays the operation of the universal joint.

The second mechanism is a double-slider coupling. A double-slider coupling is used a great deal in industrial machinery, and is sold in a large range of sizes. This coupling allows a modest amount of offset between the two shaft ends, thereby compensating for the settling of buildings and similar misalignments.

The third model is a very old design that was used in farm equipment. It is quite loosely fitted, and has the advantage of being able to operate in dirty environments that would ruin more elegant couplings.

All three of these models are useful teaching tools, and can be incorporated into your own designs.

## UNIVERSAL JOINT (ILLUS. 5-1 and 5-3)

This model consists of two sets of universal joints and an intermediate shaft that connects the driving and driven shafts. The assembly of these joints is known as a "constant-velocity" coupling, and is the normal application of the universal joint.

### Building the Mechanism

If you plane a piece of lumber about 20 inches long and 3 inches wide, you can cut all three baseplates from it. For the bearing blocks, prepare a piece about 15 inches long, and round its upper edge on the router table. This gives material for six parts, with some extra material for emergencies. The hand cranks and their handles are common to all three units, so cut a strip long enough to make these and the two crank arms for the loose-

# ASSEMBLY–UNIVERSAL JOINT

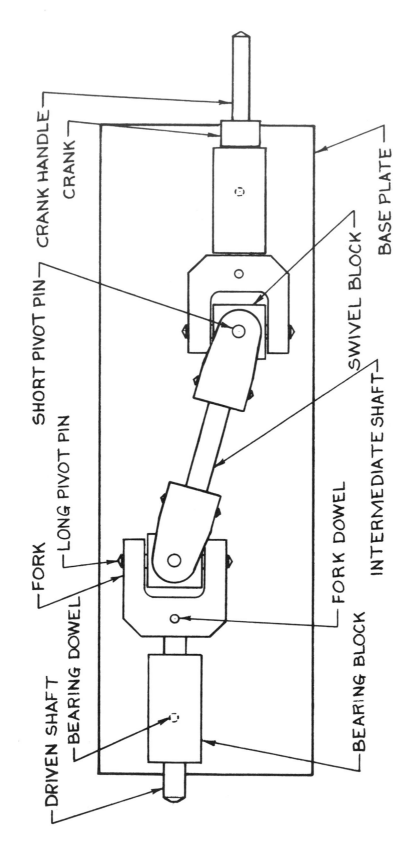

*Illus. 5-1.*

112

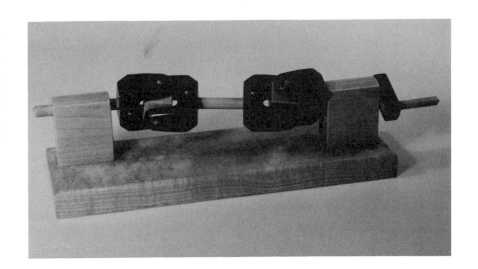

*Illus. 5-2. The Universal Joint.*

*Illus. 5-3. All the parts for the Universal Joint.*

link coupling mechanism, which have the same cross section.

Many parts in these models are similar to those in the foregoing chapters, so I won't repeat those instructions here. As always, take pains to properly fit shafts and pins to their mating parts, because the small pieces can be easily split by excessive assembly force. Size most parts so that they will fit when firmly pushed together. The glued joints should have a slightly looser fit.

113

**UNIVERSAL FORKS** Lay out the parts on a large piece of stock; keep the parts attached to the stock for as long as possible. (See Illus. 5-5.) Drill the internal corner holes and the dowel pin holes. Cut and plane the blank to its proper width and lay out the end radii and the pivot pin holes on both edges. Drill the holes. (See Illus. 5-6.)

Cut the yokes to length, and lay out and drill the shaft holes in their ends. (See Illus. 5-7.) Now, cut out the inside contours of the forks with a band saw. A ⅛-inch saw blade

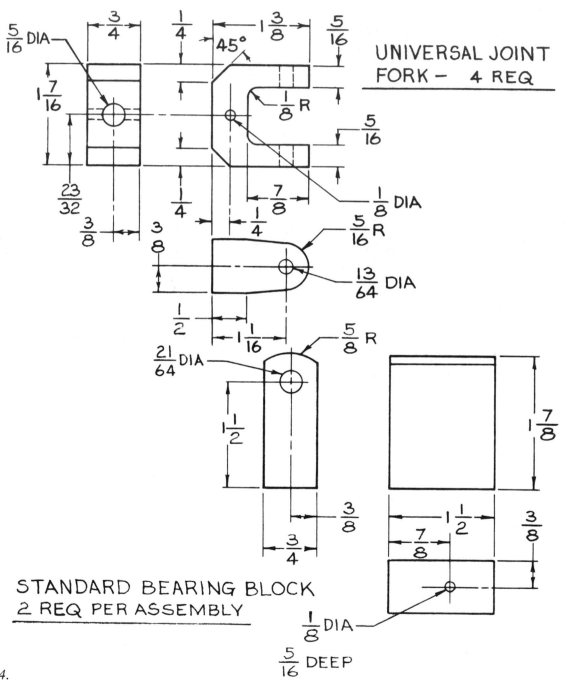

UNIVERSAL JOINT
FORK –  4 REQ

STANDARD BEARING BLOCK
2 REQ PER ASSEMBLY

*Illus. 5-4.*

*Illus. 5-5. The layout for the yokes.*

*Illus. 5-6. The yoke blanks drilled.*

*Illus. 5-7. The yokes cut to length.*

turns around nicely in the ¼-inch corner holes. Smooth the insides of the forks using a file and sandpaper, and cut the corner chamfers and the fork end radii. Lightly chamfer all sharp corners. (See Illus. 5-8.)

## THE REMAINING PARTS (ILLUS. 5-10)

The base is a simple slab with its upper corners rounded and two dowel holes in its top face. To avoid making jigs, use one dowel per block to locate the bearings, aligning the parts with a square at assembly.

Cut the bearing blocks, drilling an undersized hole from each end, and then all the way through with the full-sized drill.

Lay out the swivel blocks on a squared piece of wood and drill all the holes; plug the first hole in each block with a short piece of dowel, before drilling the crossing hole. Cut in the layout lines with a marking knife to eliminate splintering. Do all the smoothing possible at each stage of cutting, so you will have only one surface left on each small block to smooth when you make the last cut. (See Illus. 5-9.)

There are three pivot pins for each joint: one long, and two short ones. These pins must be fitted so that you can push them all the way through the blocks, or you won't be able to disassemble the model.

Fit one of the intermediate shaft ends into each of two forks, and drill through for the

*Illus. 5-8. The completed yokes.*

*Illus. 5-9. The blank for the swivel blocks, laid out and drilled.*

## DRIVEN SHAFT
$\frac{5}{16}$ DIA X 2$\frac{7}{8}$

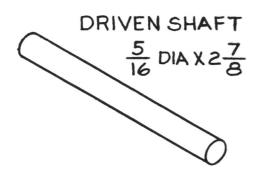

## DRIVE SHAFT
$\frac{5}{16}$ DIA X 2$\frac{13}{32}$

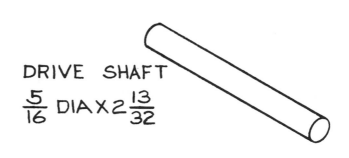

## INTERMEDIATE SHAFT
$\frac{5}{16}$ DIA X 2$\frac{1}{4}$

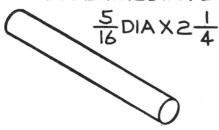

## CRANK HANDLE
$\frac{1}{4}$ DIA X 1$\frac{5}{8}$

## LONG PIVOT PIN-2 REQ
$\frac{3}{16}$ DIA X 1$\frac{9}{16}$

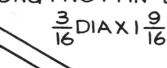

## SHORT PIVOT PIN-4 REQ
$\frac{3}{16}$ DIA X $\frac{11}{16}$

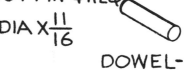

## DOWEL-
2 REQ-$\frac{1}{8}$ DIA X $\frac{9}{16}$

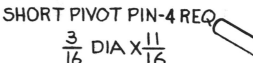

## FORK DOWEL-4 REQ
$\frac{1}{8}$ DIA X $\frac{7}{8}$

$\frac{3}{8}$

$\frac{3}{8}$

$\frac{3}{8}$

$\frac{3}{8}$

$\frac{3}{16}$ DIA

$\frac{3}{8}$ BLOCK-2REQ-
$\frac{3}{4}$ X $\frac{3}{4}$ X $\frac{3}{4}$

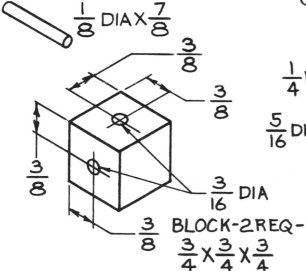

## CRANK
$\frac{1}{2}$R
$\frac{5}{16}$
$\frac{1}{4}$ DIA
$\frac{5}{16}$ DIA
$\frac{3}{8}$
$\frac{3}{8}$
$\frac{3}{8}$
1$\frac{3}{8}$
$\frac{9}{16}$
$\frac{9}{32}$

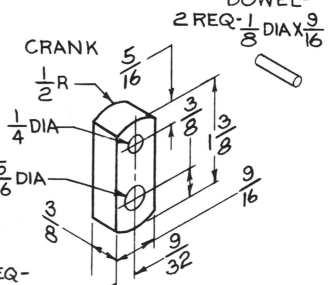

*Illus. 5-10.*

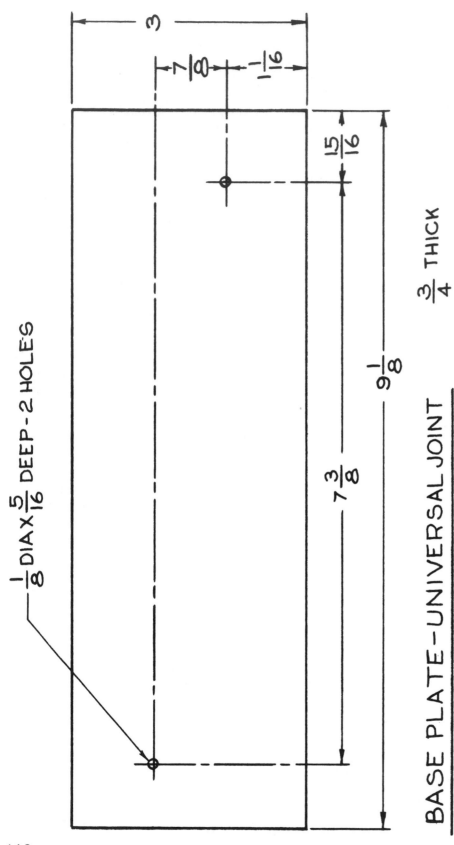

$\frac{1}{8}$ DIA $\times \frac{5}{16}$ DEEP - 2 HOLES

3

$\frac{7}{8}$

$1\frac{1}{16}$

$\frac{15}{16}$

$9\frac{1}{8}$

$7\frac{3}{8}$

$\frac{3}{4}$ THICK

BASE PLATE—UNIVERSAL JOINT

*Illus. 5-11.*

118

dowel pins. Make identifying marks to help you reassemble the parts the way they were drilled. One way is to use pencil dots on one side of each shaft, and just inside each hole. Remember, you have four shaft ends to identify at assembly, and their dowel pins probably won't go in unless the shafts are placed in their original positions.

Assemble the two remaining forks on the intermediate shaft, keeping them aligned, and drill the dowel holes. Though this member has dowels to keep things uniform, it can still be glued together, if you wish. It is, however, easier to apply a finish if the parts are all separate.

Select one of the bearing blocks for the drive end of the unit. Put the drive shaft with its fork through the hole, and push the crank onto the shaft end. Check the end play when the shaft is flush with the face of the crank; it should be about 1/64 inch or a little more. If necessary, trim the shaft or the block to achieve this fit. Make the four dowel pins. All the parts are now made. (See Illus. 5-3.)

## Assembling the Mechanism

Set the baseplate so that the dowel hole farthest from its end of the plate is to your right. Put a dowel in place and set the bearing block, to which you fitted the crankshaft, on the dowel. Check the fit, and, if satisfied, glue the block in place, aligning it with a small square while slowly tightening the clamp. Do the same with the remaining bearing block, and let the assembly dry.

Glue the crankshaft and the handle into the crank, sanding the ends of both flush with the surface when dry. Fine-sand all the parts, and apply a couple of coats of finish. Wax all the bearing surfaces.

To assemble, put the crankshaft in place and push its fork onto the inboard end, checking your alignment marks. Push in the dowel. Put the driven shaft into its bearing and assemble its fork. Make the intermediate shaft assembly of two forks and their shaft.

Hold a block in the drive-end fork and push a long pivot pin through both parts. Center the block on the pin. Do the same for the driven shaft. Now, hold the intermediate shaft assembly in position and push the two short pins into each block. This completes the assembly.

Turn the crank to test the action. The universal joints in your automobile would need replacing long before they became as loose as the ones in this model, but these clearances are just about right for a wooden coupling.

# DOUBLE-SLIDER COUPLING (ILLUS. 5-12–5-14)

This device compensates for the small misalignments that gradually appear in large machinery, especially machinery which is fastened to a building structure. With the 1/4-inch offset of the two shafts in the model, it does not seem possible that the shafts could turn; in fact, they do so quite smoothly if things are properly fitted.

*Illus. 5-12. The Double-Slider Coupling.*

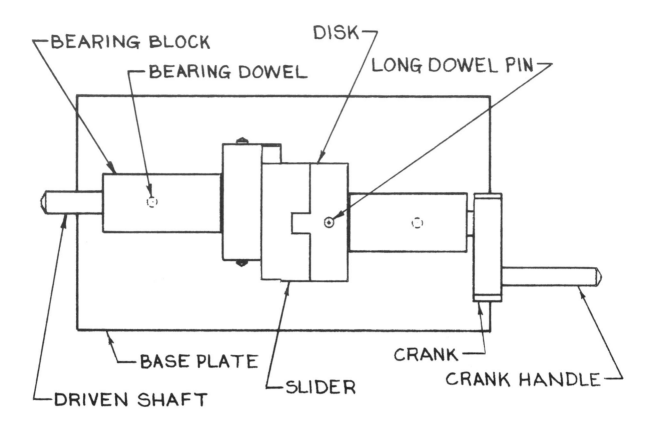

BEARING BLOCK

BEARING DOWEL

DISK

LONG DOWEL PIN

BASE PLATE

SLIDER

CRANK

CRANK HANDLE

DRIVEN SHAFT

## ASSEMBLY-DOUBLE SLIDER COUPLING

*Illus. 5-13.*

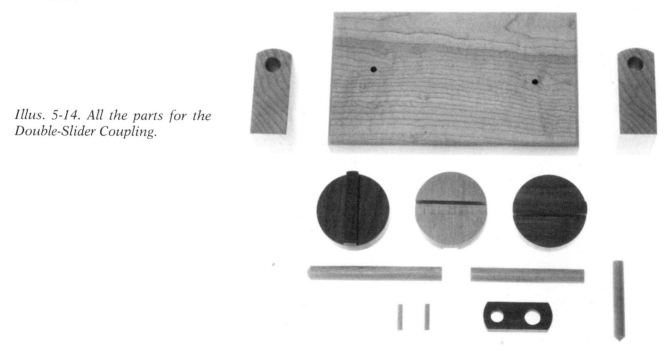

*Illus. 5-14. All the parts for the Double-Slider Coupling.*

120

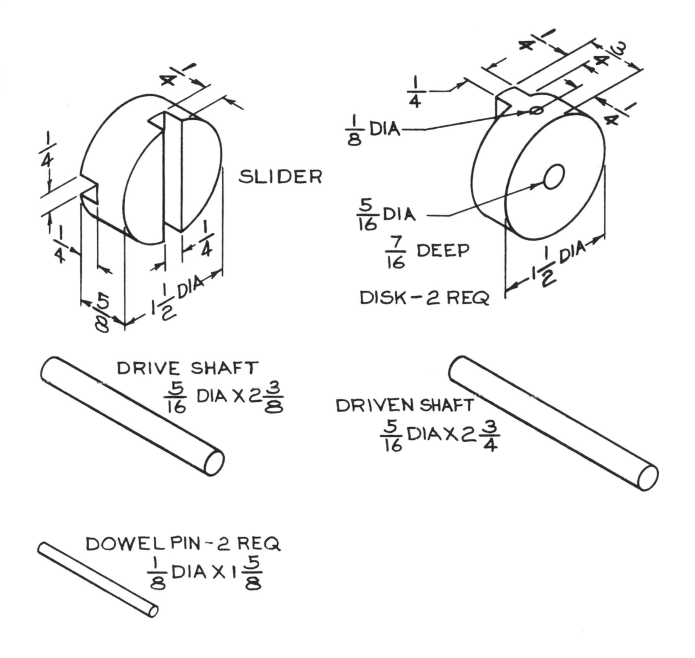

SLIDER

$\frac{1}{4}$

$\frac{1}{4}$

$\frac{1}{4}$

$\frac{1}{4}$

$\frac{5}{8}$

$1\frac{1}{2}$ DIA

$\frac{1}{4}$

$\frac{1}{4}$

$\frac{3}{4}$

$\frac{1}{4}$

$\frac{1}{8}$ DIA

$\frac{5}{16}$ DIA

$\frac{7}{16}$ DEEP

$1\frac{1}{2}$ DIA

DISK – 2 REQ

DRIVE SHAFT
$\frac{5}{16}$ DIA X $2\frac{3}{8}$

DRIVEN SHAFT
$\frac{5}{16}$ DIA X $2\frac{3}{4}$

DOWEL PIN – 2 REQ
$\frac{1}{8}$ DIA X $1\frac{5}{8}$

NOTE – BEARING BLOCKS, CRANK, HANDLE, DOWELS,
SAME AS UNIVERSAL JOINT

*Illus. 5-15.*

121

# BASE PLATE—DOUBLE SLIDER COUPLING

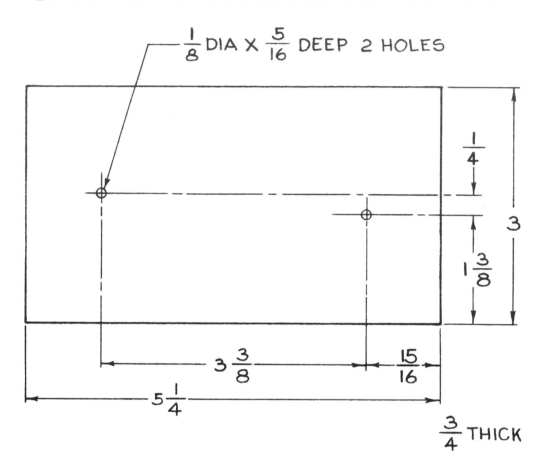

$\frac{1}{8}$ DIA X $\frac{5}{16}$ DEEP  2 HOLES

$\frac{3}{4}$ THICK

## Making the Mechanism

The bearing blocks, crank, and handle are made the same way as those parts for the Universal Joint mechanism. The baseplate is similar to that for the Universal Joint mechanism except for length and hole layout. The only new parts are the two coupling disks and the slider.

Cut rectangular blocks of the proper thickness and long enough to be safe to work on. Lay out the two slots on the piece for the slider, and the central tang on the piece for the disks. One way to cut both parts is to make multiple passes with a square-ground saw blade. In order to have a stable surface for drilling and sawing the disks, leave a

narrow bit of material on each side of the blank, outside of the final part diameter. (See Illus. 5-17.)

When the slots and tangs are cut in both blanks, mark centerlines for drawing the circular outlines. Illus. 5-18 shows a slightly tapered stick wedged into one slot in the slider piece; this provides a surface for laying out the center of the circle.

Lay out the centerline of the tangs on the blank for the disks. Square this line around to the flat face of the board, and draw the circles for the parts. Drill the shaft holes in the two disks, taking care not to break through them, and saw out the parts. Belt- or disk-sand to the lines; then fine-sand by hand in the direction of rotation. Illus. 5-19 shows a short

*Illus. 5-17. A narrow "land" on each side of the blank supports the part while it is being drilled and bandsawed.*

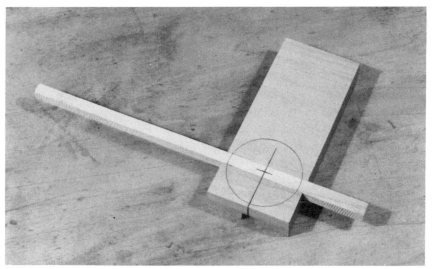

*Illus. 5-18. The stick wedged into a slot in the slider provides a surface for laying out the center.*

*Illus. 5-19. The jig for sanding the disks, clamped to the belt sander.*

123

dowel pressed into a board clamped to the sander table. I set each disk on the dowel, and tap the jig until the part makes contact with the moving belt. The part is revolved until the belt stops cutting; then I check its diameter and repeat the operation until the part is at its correct size.

Push the two shafts into their disks and drill the dowel pin holes through both members, making alignment marks as for the Universal Joint mechanism. Make the two long dowel pins, fitting them so that they enter the holes easily for about two-thirds of their lengths, and then require a light push to fully assemble.

### Assembling the Mechanism

Put the drive shaft with disk attached into its hole in the bearing block. Push the crank onto the shaft end, adjust it so that it has about ¼-inch clearance from the bearing block. Trim any excess from the end of the shaft.

Fine-sand all the parts, making certain that the two tangs on the disks slide freely in their slots in the slider. (See Illus. 5-14.) Glue the bearing blocks to the base. When the glue is dry, stack together the three parts of the coupling, and try their fit between the bearing blocks. The assembly is dimensioned for zero clearance, so your coupling may be a free fit or too large to assemble, depending on the exact sizes of all your parts.

If you have at least ¹⁄₆₄-inch clearance, apply a finish to the parts. If the parts fit together too tightly, sand a little off their various flat faces. Make sure that the tangs don't extend to the bottom of their slots in the slider.

When the proper fit is achieved, apply a finish to and wax all the parts. To assemble the coupling, push one shaft through its bearing block and into its disk, securing the assembly with one of the long dowel pins. Assemble the other disk and the slider with the first disk, and hold the parts in place while you insert the other shaft and the dowel pin. The coupling should operate smoothly despite the large offset of the shafts.

# LOOSE-LINK COUPLING
## (ILLUS. 5-20–5-22)

As stated before, this coupling will absorb a lot of dirt without becoming inoperative, and compensates for a fair amount of shaft misalignment. All parts are similar to those of the Universal Joint and Double Slider Coupling, and should require no special instruc-

*Illus. 5-20. The Loose-Link Coupling.*

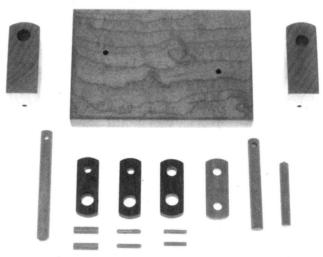

*Illus. 5-21. All the parts for the Loose-Link Coupling.*

# ASSEMBLY–LOOSE–LINK COUPLING

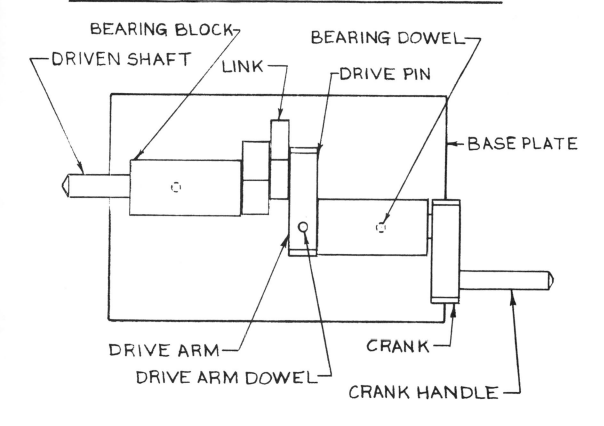

BEARING BLOCK
DRIVEN SHAFT
LINK
BEARING DOWEL
DRIVE PIN
BASE PLATE
DRIVE ARM
DRIVE ARM DOWEL
CRANK
CRANK HANDLE

*Illus. 5-22.*

# BASE PLATE–LOOSE-LINK COUPLING

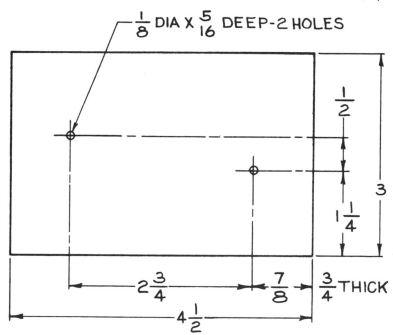

$\frac{1}{8}$ DIA X $\frac{5}{16}$ DEEP–2 HOLES

$\frac{1}{2}$

3

$1\frac{1}{4}$

$2\frac{3}{4}$

$\frac{7}{8}$

$\frac{3}{4}$ THICK

$4\frac{1}{2}$

*Illus. 5-23.*

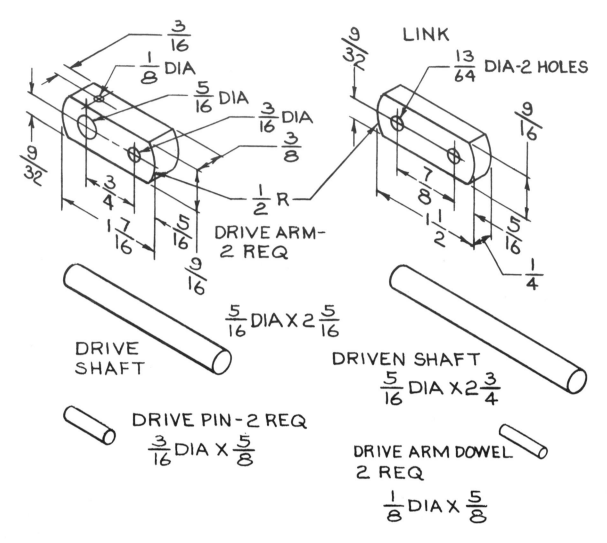

$\frac{3}{16}$

$\frac{1}{8}$ DIA

$\frac{5}{16}$ DIA

$\frac{3}{16}$ DIA

$\frac{3}{8}$

$\frac{9}{32}$

$\frac{3}{4}$

$1\frac{7}{16}$

$\frac{5}{16}$

$\frac{9}{16}$

$\frac{1}{2}$ R

DRIVE ARM—
2 REQ

LINK

$\frac{9}{32}$

$\frac{13}{64}$ DIA-2 HOLES

$\frac{9}{16}$

$\frac{7}{8}$

$1\frac{1}{2}$

$\frac{5}{16}$

$\frac{1}{4}$

$\frac{5}{16}$ DIA X $2\frac{5}{16}$

DRIVE
SHAFT

DRIVEN SHAFT
$\frac{5}{16}$ DIA X $2\frac{3}{4}$

DRIVE PIN-2 REQ
$\frac{3}{16}$ DIA X $\frac{5}{8}$

DRIVE ARM DOWEL
2 REQ
$\frac{1}{8}$ DIA X $\frac{5}{8}$

NOTE — BEARING BLOCKS, CRANK, HANDLE, DOWELS
SAME AS UNIVERSAL JOINT

*Illus. 5-24.*

tions. Adjust the end clearance of the drive shaft as before, and drill the dowel pin holes, remembering to make alignment marks.

## Assembling the Mechanism

Add dowels to the bearing blocks and glue the blocks to the base. Glue the drive shaft into the crank, and the drive pins into the arms, taking care that they extend from the proper faces. Apply a finish and wax all the parts.

Insert the drive shaft into its bearing, and

pin on the drive arm. Put the driven arm and the loose link in place, and slide the driven shaft through its bearing and into the arm, pinning it with the other dowel. You now have a coupling that will function in conditions that would defeat more sophisticated designs. The large shaft offset designed into this model gives an interesting intermittent motion to the driven shaft.

This completes the series of three different coupling mechanisms. You can build them to demonstrate their actions, or incorporate them into your own designs.

126

# CHAPTER 6
# Watt's Sun-and-Planet Motion

In 1775, when James Watt was perfecting the steam engine, the common crankshaft was thoroughly protected by someone else's patent. To avoid infringement, Watt devised this substitute, which has been named for him and is an early example of planetary, or epicyclic gearing.

## HOW THE MECHANISM WORKS

A "sun gear" is attached to the engine shaft and rotates with it. A "planet gear" is fixed to the connecting rod, and does not rotate about its own axis, but is guided in an orbital path around the sun gear. Although this mechanism is often incorrectly drawn with a connecting link, which would have infringed upon the crankshaft patent, the design that follows is an accurate reproduction of Watt's engine in that it uses a circular slot to guide the planet gear in its orbital path. A unique feature of this device is that the sun gear makes two revolutions for each orbit of the planet gear.

## MAKING THE PARTS

### Gears

Don't let the gears frighten you away from this interesting project. I have laid them out so that they are easy to make. Select a wood that is both stable and strong, as some of the gear teeth will have short grain across their narrow widths. My gears are made of applewood salvaged from a firewood pile. Cherry and similar woods are also suitable.

Photocopy the patterns shown in Illus. 6-4, checking that they are not more than full-size, and glue them to the wood. Mark each hole center with an awl, and drill all the holes, including those at the "roots" of the teeth. Accuracy is important, so try this old machinist's technique: Drill each hole sufficiently undersize so that no likely amount of error will cut into the pattern outlines. Examine each hole in turn, using a magnifier. File any hole that appears to be off-center with a small, round file, to center it. When

127

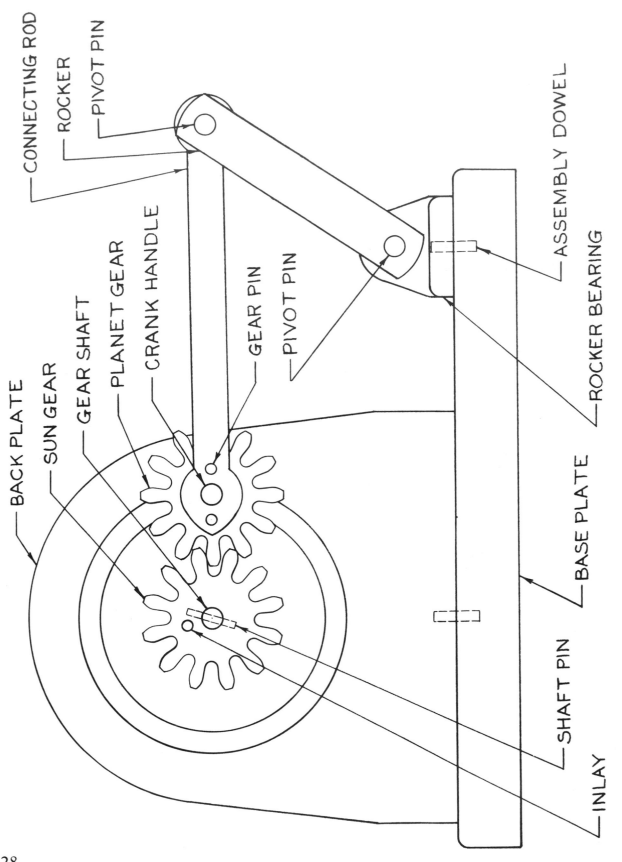

CONNECTING ROD
ROCKER
PIVOT PIN

ASSEMBLY DOWEL

BACK PLATE
SUN GEAR
GEAR SHAFT
PLANET GEAR
CRANK HANDLE
GEAR PIN
PIVOT PIN

ROCKER BEARING

BASE PLATE

SHAFT PIN

INLAY

Illus. 6-1.

128

*Illus. 6-2. Watt's Sun-and-Planet Motion.*

*Illus. 6-3. All the parts for Watt's Sun-and-Planet Motion.*

129

*Illus. 6-4.*

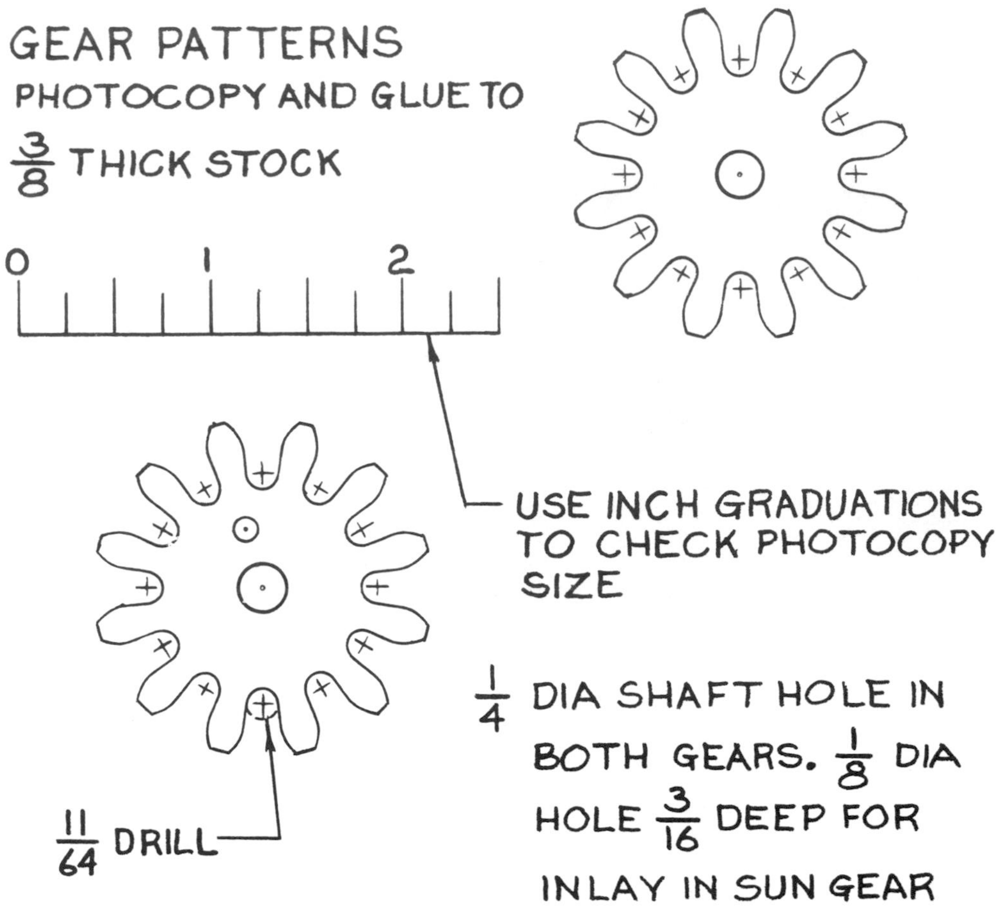

# GEAR PATTERNS
## PHOTOCOPY AND GLUE TO
## $\frac{3}{8}$ THICK STOCK

USE INCH GRADUATIONS
TO CHECK PHOTOCOPY
SIZE

$\frac{1}{4}$ DIA SHAFT HOLE IN
BOTH GEARS. $\frac{1}{8}$ DIA
HOLE $\frac{3}{16}$ DEEP FOR
INLAY IN SUN GEAR

$\frac{11}{64}$ DRILL

*Illus. 6-5. The gear patterns glued to the wood, with the holes drilled.*

130

you have done this to all holes that need it, run the final-sized drill through each hole. You can do very accurate work this way. (See Illus. 6-5.)

Saw the gears to circular disks, and then sand them round and smooth. One way to sand them is to rotate them on a dowel in a block clamped to a belt sander, and tap them slowly into the belt to produce the desired diameter. Saw the teeth as close to the lines as you safely can. (See Illus. 6-6.) If you own a jigsaw, you can produce almost finished teeth on it.

Remove any remaining material with a small file, splitting or even removing the pattern lines. If you own a machinist's slide caliper, you can use it to get all the teeth to the same thickness. Remove the patterns, and lightly round all sharp corners. (See Illus. 6-7.)

*Illus. 6-6. Cutting out the tooth profiles with a band saw.*

*Illus. 6-7. The completed gears.*

## Backplate

While the circular groove can be plowed out of a solid block on a lathe, it is far better to use the built-up construction shown in Illus. 6-10, as it makes it easier to fine-sand the bearing surfaces of the groove.

You will need two razor-sharp tool bits for the circle cutter. If you do not have much experience using the circle cutter, review the equipment section. Plane the two thicknesses of stock for the backplate, and make the layout on the thin front member. Clamp the two blanks together and drill the center hole through them using the same size drill as is in your circle cutter. (See Illus. 6-8.)

*Illus. 6-8. The two blanks for the backplate.*

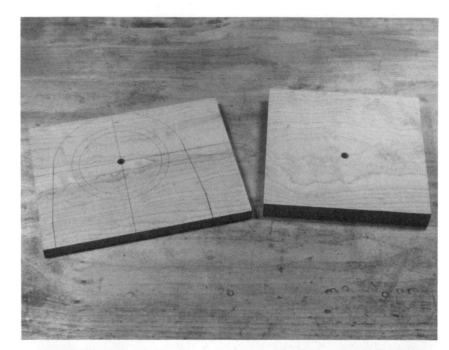

*Illus. 6-9. Cutting the disk on the drill press.*

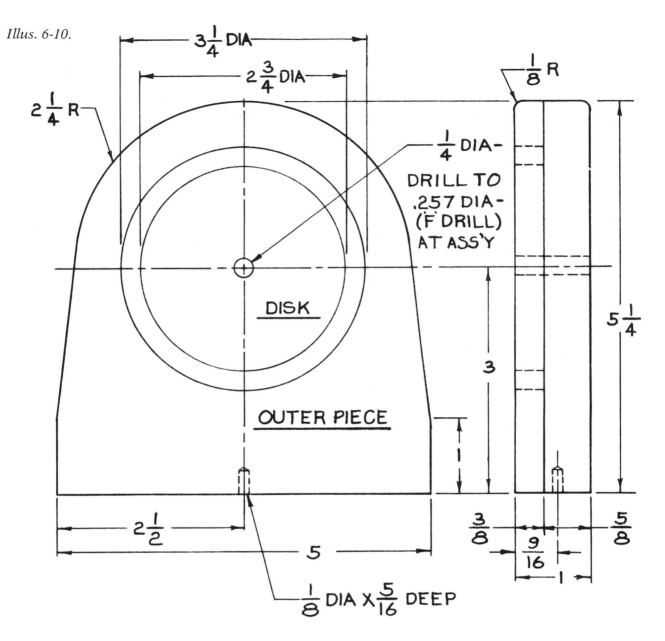

*Illus. 6-10.*

$3\frac{1}{4}$ DIA

$2\frac{3}{4}$ DIA

$2\frac{1}{4}$ R

$\frac{1}{8}$ R

$\frac{1}{4}$ DIA-

DRILL TO
.257 DIA-
(F DRILL)
AT ASS'Y

DISK

OUTER PIECE

$5\frac{1}{4}$

3

$2\frac{1}{2}$

5

$\frac{3}{8}$

$\frac{9}{16}$

$\frac{5}{8}$

1

$\frac{1}{8}$ DIA X $\frac{5}{16}$ DEEP

SEQUENCE FOR BACK PLATE
1- LAY OUT ON $\frac{3}{8}$ THICK STOCK
2- CLAMP BOTH BLANKS TOGETHER AND DRILL $\frac{1}{4}$ HOLE
3- CUT DISK AND LARGE HOLE TO SIZE
4- GLUE DISK TO REAR MEMBER
5- GLUE OUTER PIECE TO REAR MEMBER
6- DRILL CENTER HOLE WITH "F"(.257) DRILL
7- CUT TO OUTLINE

133

Securely fasten the thinner piece to a backing block, line up its center hole with the pilot drill, and clamp the work to the drill-press table, where it must remain undisturbed until both cuts are completed.

Put a disk-cutting bit in the circle cutter, and adjust it to the inner radius of the groove. Make sure that if the cut isn't precise that the radius is oversize rather than undersize.

Some extra center distance won't affect the gears, but too close a distance will require you to rework all the teeth. Make the cut using a slow, steady feed rate. Your disk should require only fine-sanding to be ready for use. (See Illus. 6-9.)

Change to the hole-cutting bit and adjust it to the outer-groove radius; again, any errors should be on the "plus" side. Make the cut

*Illus. 6-11. Boring the large hole to size.*

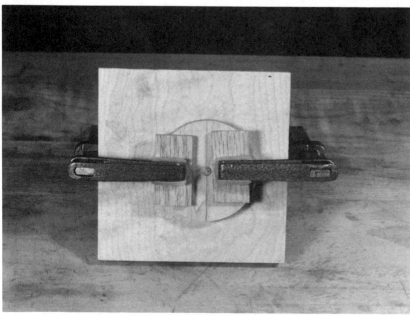

*Illus. 6-12. Gluing the disk in place.*

134

and remove the work from the drill press. (See Illus. 6-11.)

Using a piece of dowel as an alignment pin, glue the disk onto the rear member. Align the grain in its original direction. (See Illus. 6-12.) Remove the dowel before the glue sets or you may have to drill it out with a piece of dowel.

When the glue is dry, cut six spacers of a size that will fit snugly in the groove between the parts. As dowel stock is rarely round, I plane a flat on a length of 5/16-inch dowel which I then cut into six pieces. This way I can control the geometry of the spacers.

Apply glue to the parts, keeping it well away from the groove, and assemble the unit with the six dowels equally spaced. (See Illus. 6-13.) Use several clamps to keep the thin plate flat. When it is dry, cut the part to shape, sand it smooth, and round the corners. Drill the one dowel hole in the base and open the shaft hole to its finished size.

## Remaining Parts

The remaining parts are similar to those in preceding designs and don't need much ex-

planation here. Just remember the overall rule for small parts: Plan your work so that as many operations as possible can be performed with the piece still attached to a larger blank.

You may notice that the rocker bearing, the connecting rod, and the slots in the rocker are all the same thickness, which would give zero clearance. There should be very little lateral shake in this assembly, so just sand the completed parts so that they fit freely. Details for slotting the rocker are covered in the instructions for the Slide, in Chapter Four. (See Illus. 6-3.)

## ASSEMBLING THE MECHANISM

When all parts have been fitted and finish-sanded, dry-assemble the backplate to the base, using the one locating dowel. Align the part carefully and clamp a scrap block against it to provide a reference surface for final assembly. Remove the backplate, apply glue, and clamp the assembly.

After a minute or two to make certain that none of the parts will move, remove the

135

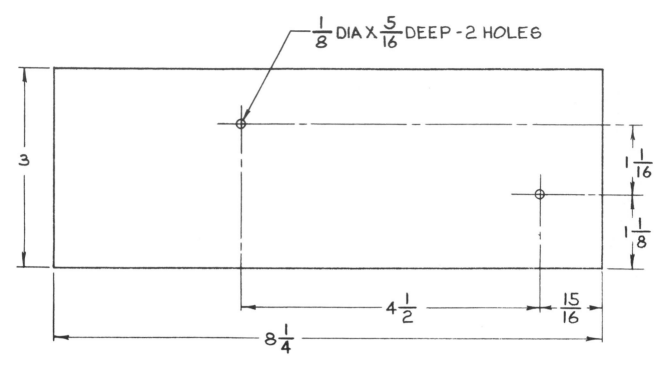

$\frac{1}{8}$ DIA X $\frac{5}{16}$ DEEP - 2 HOLES

3

$1\frac{1}{16}$

$1\frac{1}{8}$

$4\frac{1}{2}$

$\frac{15}{16}$

$8\frac{1}{4}$

BASE PLATE $\frac{3}{4}$ THICK

*Illus. 6-14.*

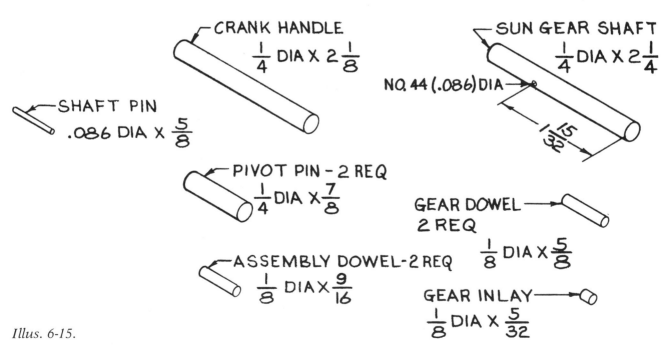

CRANK HANDLE
$\frac{1}{4}$ DIA X $2\frac{1}{8}$

SUN GEAR SHAFT
$\frac{1}{4}$ DIA X $2\frac{1}{4}$

NO. 44 (.086) DIA

SHAFT PIN
.086 DIA X $\frac{5}{8}$

$\frac{15}{32}$

PIVOT PIN - 2 REQ
$\frac{1}{4}$ DIA X $\frac{7}{8}$

GEAR DOWEL
2 REQ

$\frac{1}{8}$ DIA X $\frac{5}{8}$

ASSEMBLY DOWEL - 2 REQ
$\frac{1}{8}$ DIA X $\frac{9}{16}$

GEAR INLAY
$\frac{1}{8}$ DIA X $\frac{5}{32}$

*Illus. 6-15.*

136

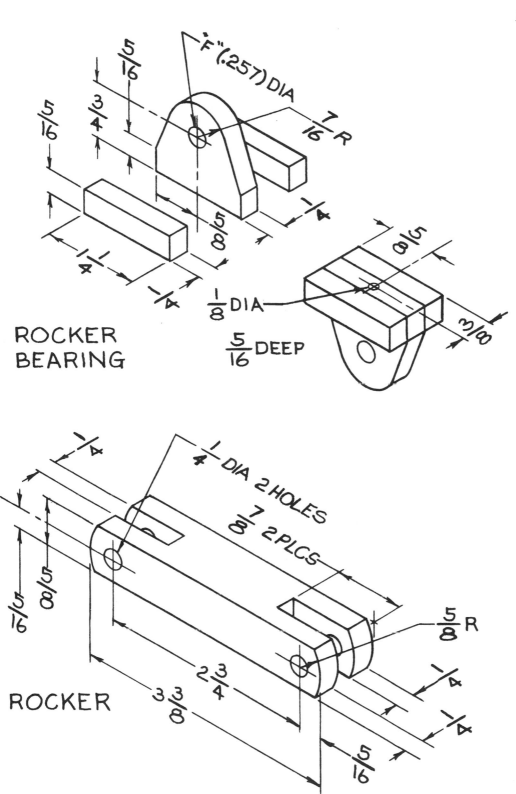

$\frac{5}{16}$

$\frac{3}{4}$

$\frac{5}{16}$

"F"(.257) DIA

$\frac{7}{16}$ R

$\frac{5}{8}$

$\frac{1}{4}$

$\frac{1}{4}$

$\frac{1}{4}$

$\frac{5}{8}$

$\frac{1}{8}$ DIA

$\frac{3}{8}$

**ROCKER BEARING**

$\frac{5}{16}$ DEEP

$\frac{1}{4}$

$\frac{1}{4}$ DIA 2 HOLES

$\frac{7}{8}$ 2 PLCS

$\frac{5}{8}$

$\frac{5}{16}$

$\frac{5}{8}$ R

$\frac{1}{4}$

$\frac{1}{4}$

$2\frac{3}{4}$

$3\frac{3}{8}$

$\frac{5}{16}$

**ROCKER**

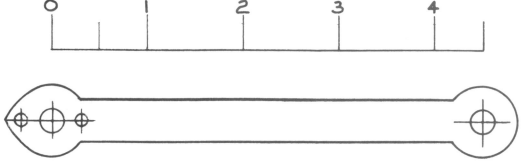

## PATTERN FOR CONNECTING ROD
### GLUE PHOTOCOPY TO $\frac{1}{4}$ INCH STOCK
### USE INCH GRADUATIONS TO CHECK COPY SIZE

### LARGE HOLES "F" DRILL (.257)
### SMALL HOLES $\frac{1}{8}$ DIA

*Illus. 6-18. Gluing the back to the base, using an aligning block.*

alignment block. (See Illus. 6-18.) Repeat this operation for the rocker bearing. Your base assembly is now complete.

Glue a contrasting colored pin into the sun gear and sand it flush. This makes it easy to count revolutions when demonstrating the

device. Fit the crank handle into the planet gear so that it can be tapped in with a small mallet; glue will be too messy here. The handle should project $1\frac{1}{32}$ inch from the back of the gear.

Put the connecting rod on the handle, and

138

line up the two dowel holes on the centerline of the rod. Drill through the dowel holes to provide a snug fit for two dowels, and tap them in. The absence of glue in this unit permits disassembly if necessary.

Pin the rocker to the connecting rod with one of the pivot pins. Set the projecting part of the crank handle into the groove, swing the rocker onto its bearing, and insert the remaining pivot pin. Try the assembly. If the gears are tight at any position, mark them and remove a little material to ease the action. When everything works smoothly, you will have an interesting and unusual model to demonstrate.

# CHAPTER 7

# The Geneva Wheel

This device converts continuous rotary input motion into intermittent output motion, the driven member being prevented from moving except when actually driven. You can find this movement in better-quality spring-wound watches, where it is used to prevent over-winding of the mainspring. In this application, one of the slots is left uncut, and the device is known as the Geneva Stop. At the other extreme, we once built a pair of these units, about 30 inches in diameter, for a glass-bottle sealing machine.

## HOW THE MECHANISM WORKS

During most of the operating cycle, the circular part of the locking disk turns in one of the semicircular cuts on the wheel, thereby preventing the wheel from moving. As the driving pin enters a slot in the wheel, the corner of the wheel is opposite a clearance cut in the locking disk, allowing the wheel to turn. Just before the pin exits the slot, the wheel is once again locked by the disk.

*Illus. 7-1. The Geneva Wheel assembled.*

Illus. 7-2.

# ASSEMBLY—GENEVA WHEEL

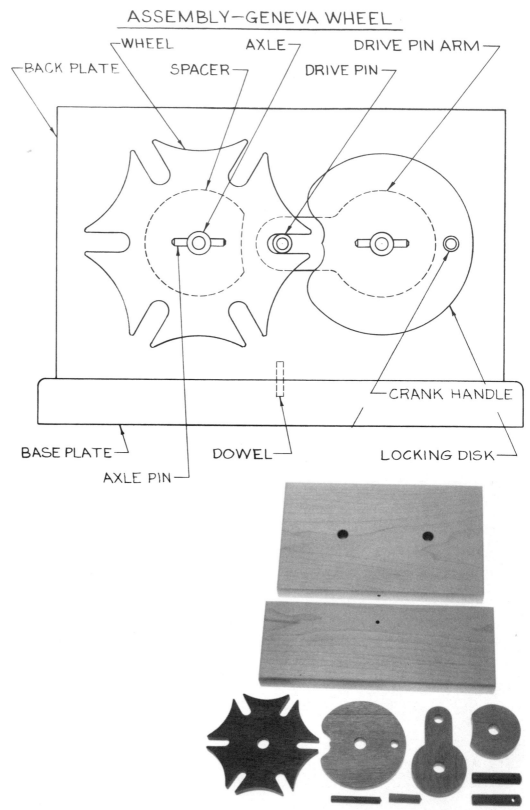

BACK PLATE

WHEEL  AXLE  DRIVE PIN ARM

SPACER  DRIVE PIN

BASE PLATE

AXLE PIN

DOWEL

CRANK HANDLE

LOCKING DISK

Illus. 7-3. All the parts for the Geneva Wheel.

## MAKING THE PARTS

The back- and baseplates, shown in Illus. 7-4 and 7-5, are similar to those of earlier models, and don't require further explanation, except to state that the hole-center distance is fairly critical, and determines the smoothness of operation of the model.

Glue the photocopied patterns to the parts (Illus. 7-6–7-8), drill all the holes, and cut out the profiles. (See Illus. 7-10.) There is a preferred sequence for making the wheel. First, drill all the holes and cut to the outline on a band saw, but don't cut the slots. Use a sanding drum in the drill press (a drum two inches in diameter is ideal) and sand the semicircular locking radii, finishing with the finest available grit of sandpaper. Sand to just remove the lines. Put the part aside until you have made the locking disk. (See Illus. 7-11.) Drill the center hole in the disk ⅜ inch

in diameter; it will be enlarged after assembly. Sand the disk to size. The best way to do this is to rotate it on a moveable pin clamped to the belt sander. Fine-sand by hand in the direction of rotation. The contours of the clearance cut can be smoothed with a sandpaper-wrapped dowel rotated at high speed in the drill press.

Drill the two axle holes in the backplate and insert pieces of dowel to serve as temporary axles. Put the locking disk on one axle, with its circular profile facing the other axle, and clamp the disk to the backplate. Now, try the wheel in all six possible positions, sanding where required so that all the locking cut-outs have equal clearance. Unless you keep this model in an environment with a very uniform humidity, you should allow a minimum of 1/64-inch clearance at each position. When you are satisfied with the fits of the locking cuts, cut the six driving slots,

*Illus. 7-4.*

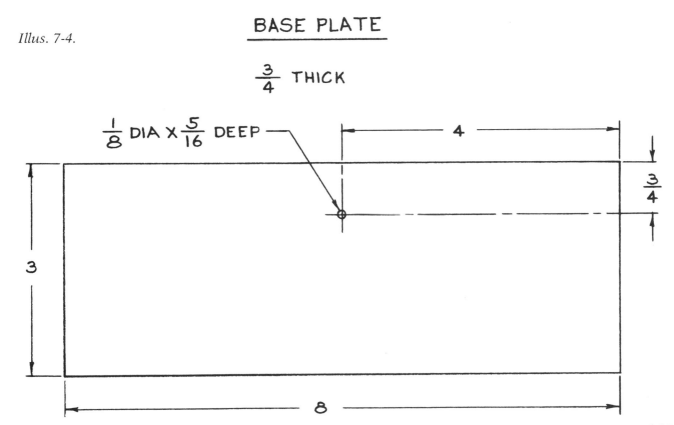

BASE PLATE

$\frac{3}{4}$ THICK

$\frac{1}{8}$ DIA X $\frac{5}{16}$ DEEP

4

3

$\frac{3}{4}$

8

# BACK PLATE

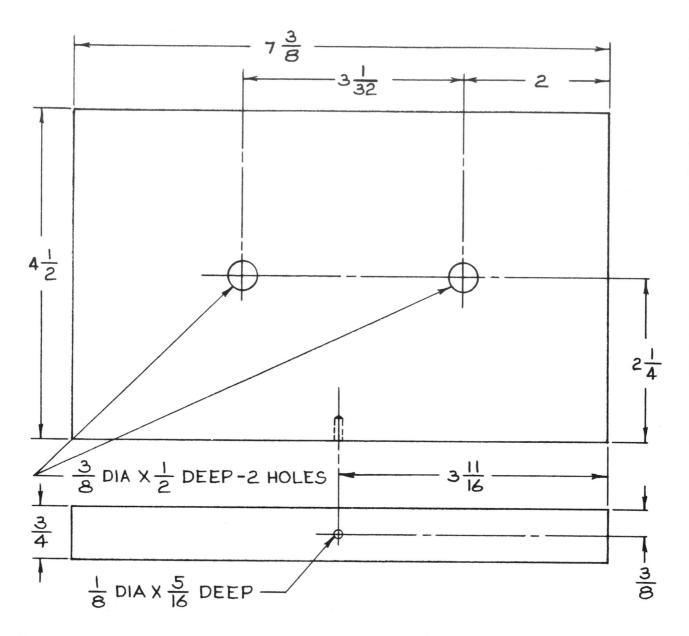

$7\frac{3}{8}$

$3\frac{1}{32}$

2

$4\frac{1}{2}$

$2\frac{1}{4}$

$\frac{3}{8}$ DIA X $\frac{1}{2}$ DEEP -2 HOLES

$3\frac{11}{16}$

$\frac{3}{4}$

$\frac{3}{8}$

$\frac{1}{8}$ DIA X $\frac{5}{16}$ DEEP

*Illus. 7-5.*

144

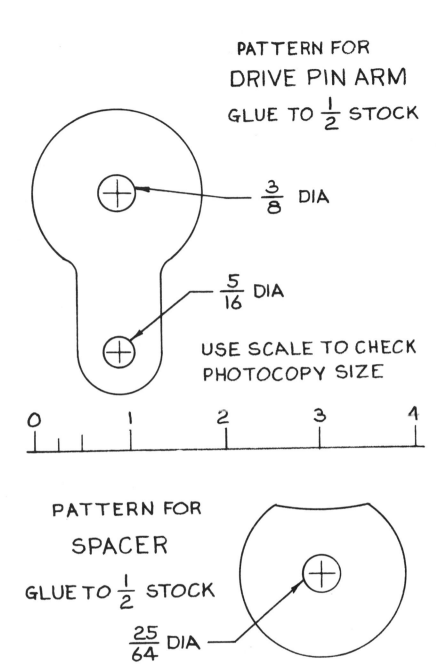

PATTERN FOR
DRIVE PIN ARM
GLUE TO $\frac{1}{2}$ STOCK

$\frac{3}{8}$ DIA

$\frac{5}{16}$ DIA

USE SCALE TO CHECK
PHOTOCOPY SIZE

0   1   2   3   4

PATTERN FOR
SPACER
GLUE TO $\frac{1}{2}$ STOCK

$\frac{25}{64}$ DIA

*Illus. 7-6.*

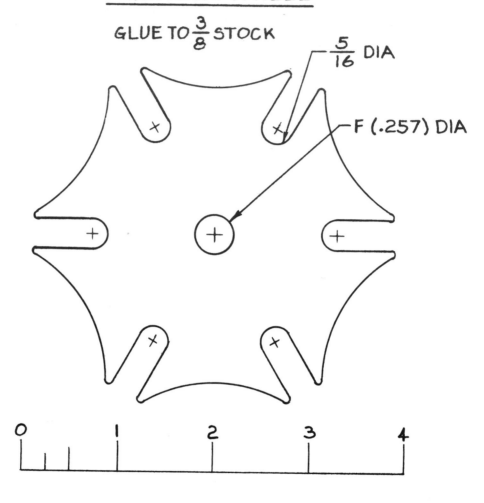

# PATTERN FOR

## GENEVA WHEEL

GLUE TO $\frac{3}{8}$ STOCK

$\frac{5}{16}$ DIA

F (.257) DIA

0   1   2   3   4

INCH SCALE TO CHECK PHOTOCOPY SIZE

Illus. 7-7.

146

# PATTERN FOR
# LOCKING DISK
### GLUE TO $\frac{3}{8}$ INCH STOCK

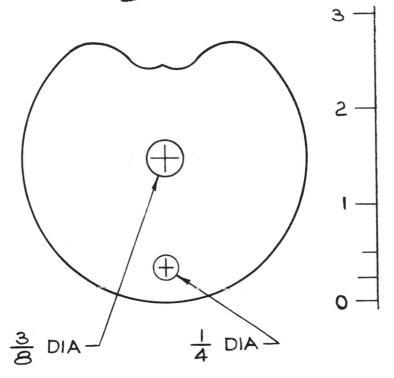

3 —

2 —

1 —

0 —

$\frac{3}{8}$ DIA —

$\frac{1}{4}$ DIA —

## USE 3 INCH SCALE TO CHECK PHOTOCOPY SIZE

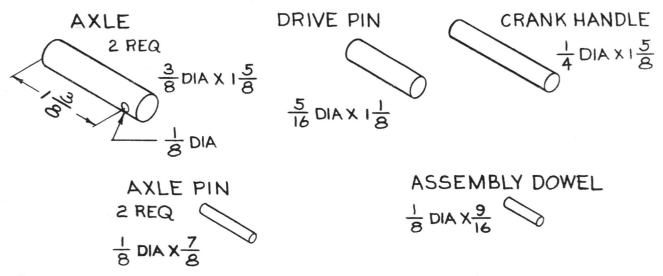

AXLE
2 REQ
$\frac{3}{8}$ DIA X $1\frac{5}{8}$
$\frac{1}{8}$ DIA

DRIVE PIN
$\frac{5}{16}$ DIA X $1\frac{1}{8}$

CRANK HANDLE
$\frac{1}{4}$ DIA X $1\frac{5}{8}$

AXLE PIN
2 REQ
$\frac{1}{8}$ DIA X $\frac{7}{8}$

ASSEMBLY DOWEL
$\frac{1}{8}$ DIA X $\frac{9}{16}$

*Illus. 7-10. The wheel pattern glued to the wood, with its holes drilled.*

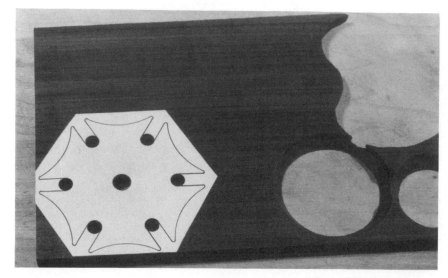

*Illus. 7-11. The wheel cut out, and its outer contour completed.*

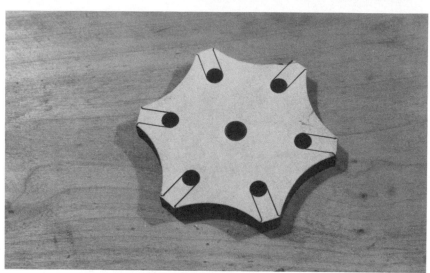

filing them to size and checking each with a piece of dowel to ensure uniform clearance. The small radii at the entrance to each slot are important, since they compensate for looseness in the assembly, and allow the drive pin to enter the slots. Fine-sand the wheel all over. (See Illus. 7-12)

Use the patterns shown in Illus. 7-6 to make the drive-pin arm and the wheel spacer. When the drive-pin arm is completed, glue it to the locking disk, using an easy-fitting, waxed dowel for an alignment tool. Center the arm in the clearance cut by eye. When the

parts are dry, run a 25/64-inch-diameter drill through them. (See Illus. 7-13.)

Make the back- and baseplates with the same techniques used for the other models. The small parts also require no additional instructions. (See Illus. 7-3.)

## ASSEMBLING THE MECHANISM

Glue the back-to-base subassembly, using an aligning block as described for other projects. Glue the spacer to the backplate, with the

*Illus. 7-12. The completed Geneva Wheel.*

*Illus. 7-13. The locking disk and the drive-arm subassembly.*

*Illus. 7-14. The back and base subassembly.*

149

clearance cut facing the locking disk; use a dowel for alignment of the parts. (See Illus. 7-14.) Glue the drive pin and the handle into the locking disk assembly. Now, dry-assemble the parts to try their operation. If any of the parts fit too tightly, sand them carefully to ease the action.

Clean up all parts and apply a finish. I tap slightly tapered dowels into the axle holes to keep the finish out of them, wiggling them out before rubbing down the coats of finish. Wax all the working surfaces and assemble the model. This is one of our more popular designs and always attracts attention.

# CHAPTER 8

# An Intermittent Drive

Various mechanisms are used to convert continuous rotary motion into intermittent rotary motion, but few are as simple as this one. This unit will drive for half a revolution, pause for an equal length of time, and then drive another half revolution, providing a useful action for display turntables, rotary valves, and similar applications.

## HOW THE MECHANISM WORKS

The drive member and the driven member have their centers offset from one another, so the part diameters are eccentric. A tang projecting from the driver engages a lug on the rotor at the close point of eccentricity, and releases it half a revolution later. The unit can be designed so that either the inner or the outer member is the driver, and works best for frictional loads that don't tend to drift or coast.

*Illus. 8-1. The Intermittent Drive.*

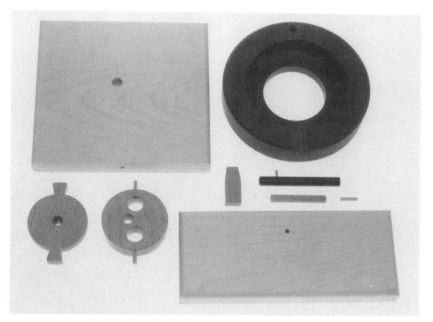

*Illus. 8-2. All the parts for the Intermittent Drive.*

# ASSEMBLY-INTERMITTENT DRIVE

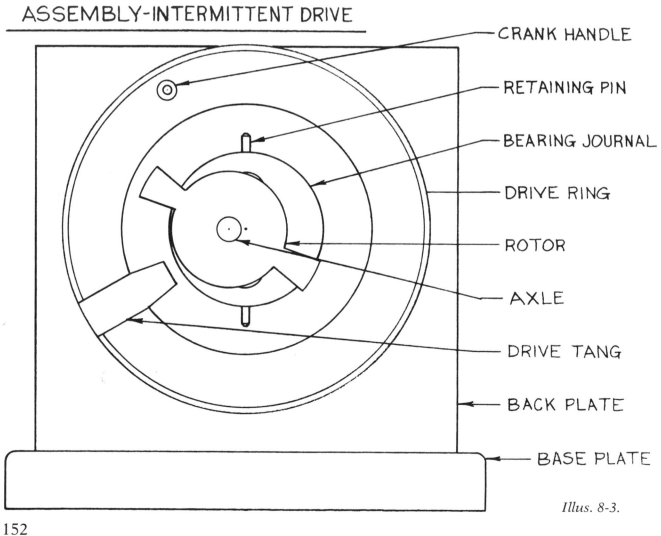

CRANK HANDLE

RETAINING PIN

BEARING JOURNAL

DRIVE RING

ROTOR

AXLE

DRIVE TANG

BACK PLATE

BASE PLATE

*Illus. 8-3.*

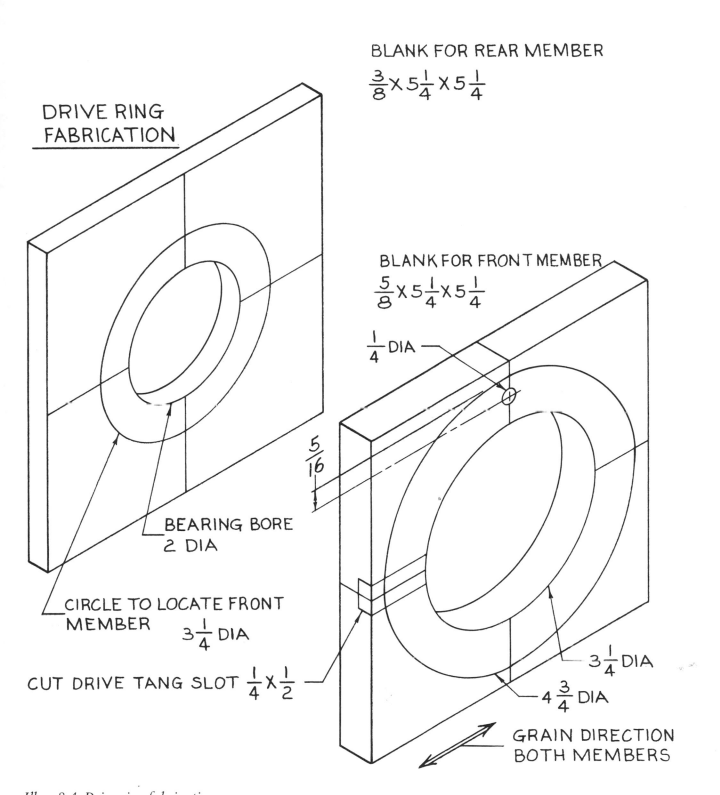

DRIVE RING
FABRICATION

BLANK FOR REAR MEMBER
$\frac{3}{8} \times 5\frac{1}{4} \times 5\frac{1}{4}$

BLANK FOR FRONT MEMBER
$\frac{5}{8} \times 5\frac{1}{4} \times 5\frac{1}{4}$

$\frac{1}{4}$ DIA

$\frac{5}{16}$

BEARING BORE
2 DIA

CIRCLE TO LOCATE FRONT
MEMBER $3\frac{1}{4}$ DIA

CUT DRIVE TANG SLOT $\frac{1}{4} \times \frac{1}{2}$

$3\frac{1}{4}$ DIA

$4\frac{3}{4}$ DIA

GRAIN DIRECTION
BOTH MEMBERS

*Illus. 8-4. Drive ring fabrication.*

# MAKING THE PARTS

## Drive Ring

The two-piece drive ring requires a sharp circle cutter for its two large holes. Plane the two thicknesses of stock and lay out the circles as shown in Illus. 8-4. Fasten each piece to a backing block and cut the two inside diameters. Sand the holes smooth, as they will be difficult to sand after gluing the assembly.

Lay out the slot for the drive tang so that it is parallel to one smooth edge of the blank and aligned with the grain. Cut the slot on a router table or a table saw. Lay out and drill the hole for the crank handle.

Apply glue to both pieces, keeping it well away from the inner edge of the large hole. Align the front member with the circle drawn on the rear member, checking constantly while clamping to see that nothing shifts. If any glue squeezes inside the hole, remove it immediately with a wet cloth, so the alignment circle is not obscured. (See Illus. 8-5.)

Allow the joint a day or two to dry and then saw and sand the outer diameter. The corner chamfers enhance the part's appearance, and can be easily cut on a router table. To avoid chipping the corners, plug the slot with a tight-fitting piece of scrap wood, as shown in Illus. 8-7. Clamp a stop block to the router table, square to the fence and placed so as to center the disk on a chamfering bit. Rotate the part into the revolving cutter. This is a quick, safe way to cut the chamfers.

## Bearing Journal (Illus. 8-6)

With the driver ring completed, you can make the bearing journal so that it fits the center hole. Allow at least 1/64-inch clearance for seasonal changes. Drill the three holes in the face, and the two pin holes in the edge. Before drilling the pin holes, check the thickness of the rear member of the driver assembly. If this varies much from 3/8 inch, adjust the pin-hole locations to provide a small amount of operating clearance when the parts are assembled. (See Illus. 8-8.)

## Remaining Parts (Illus. 8-9)

The rest of the pieces are similar to others in earlier projects and should present no problems. Fit the two retaining pins so that, when

*Illus. 8-5. The drive-ring parts glued together.*

154

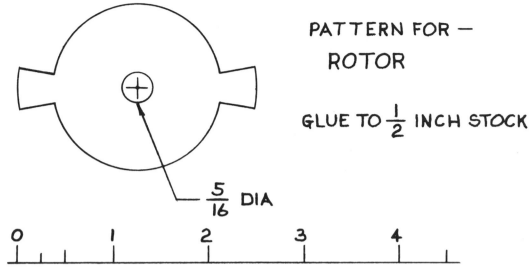

*Illus. 8-6.*

PATTERN FOR —
ROTOR

GLUE TO $\frac{1}{2}$ INCH STOCK

$\frac{5}{16}$ DIA

INCH SCALE – USE TO CHECK PHOTOCOPY SIZE

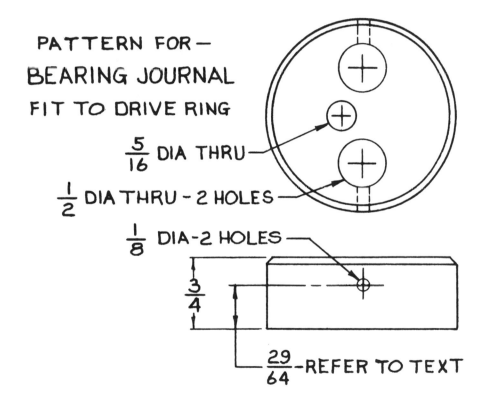

PATTERN FOR —
BEARING JOURNAL
FIT TO DRIVE RING

$\frac{5}{16}$ DIA THRU

$\frac{1}{2}$ DIA THRU - 2 HOLES

$\frac{1}{8}$ DIA - 2 HOLES

$\frac{3}{4}$

$\frac{29}{64}$ – REFER TO TEXT

*Illus. 8-7. The setup for cutting a chamfer on the drive ring.*

*Illus. 8-8. The bearing journal.*

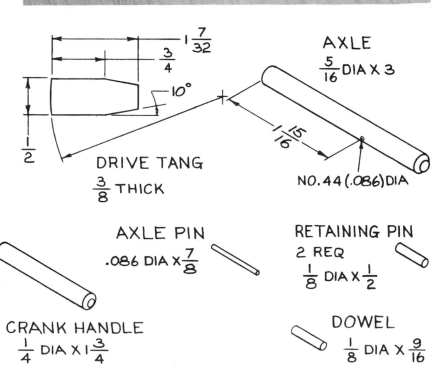

*Illus. 8-9.*

DRIVE TANG
$\frac{3}{8}$ THICK

$1\frac{7}{32}$

$\frac{3}{4}$

10°

$\frac{1}{2}$

AXLE
$\frac{5}{16}$ DIA X 3

$1\frac{15}{16}$

NO. 44 (.086) DIA

AXLE PIN
.086 DIA X $\frac{7}{8}$

RETAINING PIN
2 REQ
$\frac{1}{8}$ DIA X $\frac{1}{2}$

CRANK HANDLE
$\frac{1}{4}$ DIA X $1\frac{3}{4}$

DOWEL
$\frac{1}{8}$ DIA X $\frac{9}{16}$

156

# BACK PLATE

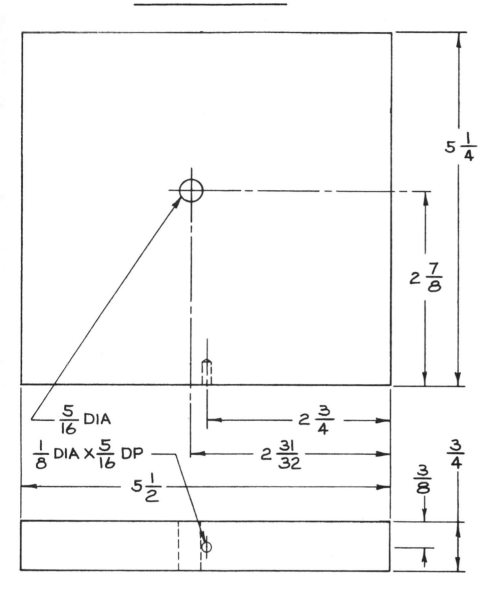

$5\frac{1}{4}$

$2\frac{7}{8}$

$\frac{5}{16}$ DIA

$\frac{1}{8}$ DIA $\times \frac{5}{16}$ DP

$5\frac{1}{2}$

$2\frac{3}{4}$

$2\frac{31}{32}$

$\frac{3}{8}$

$\frac{3}{4}$

finished and waxed, they can be pushed in and out of engagement without a lot of effort. Make the drive tang a snug fit in its slot and use the pattern in Illus. 8-6 to make the rotor. (See Illus. 8-2.)

## Assembling the Unit

Glue the back to the base, and glue the journal to the backplate, using a waxed dowel for alignment. When the parts are dry, drill the shaft hole to a 21/64-inch diameter.

Glue the tang into the driver and sand it flush if necessary to match the outer radius. Glue the axle into the rotor so that the axle pin clears the backplate when assembled, and sand the end flush with the front face. Glue the crank handle into the driver. Clean up and apply a finish to all the parts.

Push the two retaining pins flush with the

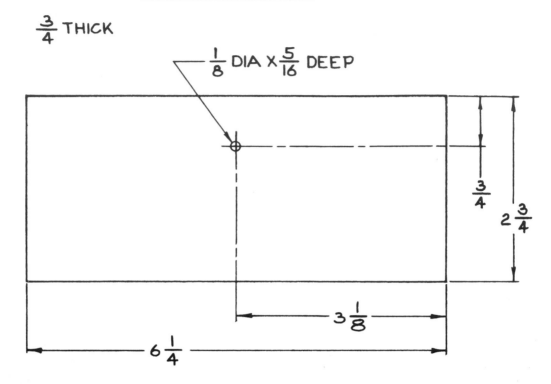

## BASE PLATE

$\frac{3}{4}$ THICK

$\frac{1}{8}$ DIA X $\frac{5}{16}$ DEEP

$\frac{3}{4}$

$2\frac{3}{4}$

$3\frac{1}{8}$

$6\frac{1}{4}$

diameter of the bearing journal. Wax all the rubbing surfaces, set the driver in place, and push the two pins outward to retain it. The driver should turn freely, with a minimum of shake. Assemble the rotor and its pin, completing the assembly.

For each full turn of the crank handle, the rotor will make half a revolution, a useful action for a variety of toy and display designs.

# CHAPTER 9

# Positive-Action Cam

This is another form of self-conjugate cam. Unlike the one in Chapter 2, which was intended for a particular application, this type of cam permits greater flexibility in its design, and is more often used in industrial machinery.

In this model, I include two interchangeable cam profiles; you can also use cams of your own design.

## HOW THE MECHANISM WORKS

The cam operates between rollers mounted on a follower slide and contacts both rollers throughout its rotation. Therefore, no external force is required to keep the follower against the cam, so this mechanism will function in any position and is not subject to "follower float" at high operating speeds.

*Illus. 9-1. A front view of the Positive-Action Cam.*

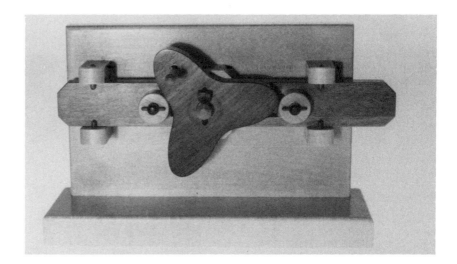

*Illus. 9-2. A rear view of the Positive-Action Cam.*

*Illus. 9-3. All the parts for the Positive-Action Cam.*

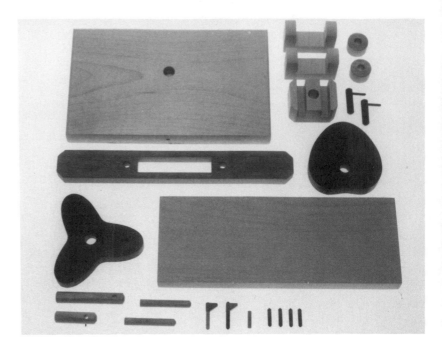

*Illus. 9-4.*

# ASSEMBLY-POSITIVE ACTION CAM

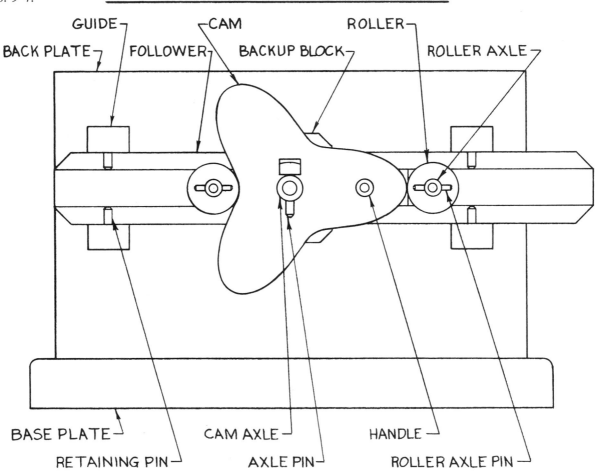

## MAKING THE PARTS

### Back- and Baseplates

Make the back- and baseplates as shown in Illus. 9-5 and 9-7. The hole on the rear of the backplate is for a parking axle to hold the second cam, and may be omitted if you only intend to make one cam.

### Follower Slide (Illus. 9-6)

Cut the four pieces of this part a little longer than finished size and glue them together, leaving the correct length of opening in the center. (See Illus. 9-8.) When they are dry, trim the part to size and shape and drill the two roller axle holes, locating them as accurately as you can.

### Follower Guides (Illus. 9-6)

Cut material long enough to make several parts, and glue it together as shown in Illus. 9-9. The center block should be slightly larger than the follower, to allow this part to slide easily.
· Slice off the two guides and sand them clean. Lay out and drill the pin holes, locating them so as to allow slight clearance for the thickness of the slide.

### Cam Backup Block (Illus 9-6)

This part is also built up from pieces. Drill the axle hole in the center member before gluing the assembly, to avoid losing the whole block if the drill wanders. Glue the pieces and trim them to size when they are dry. The height of the block should position the cam just above the slide to prevent these

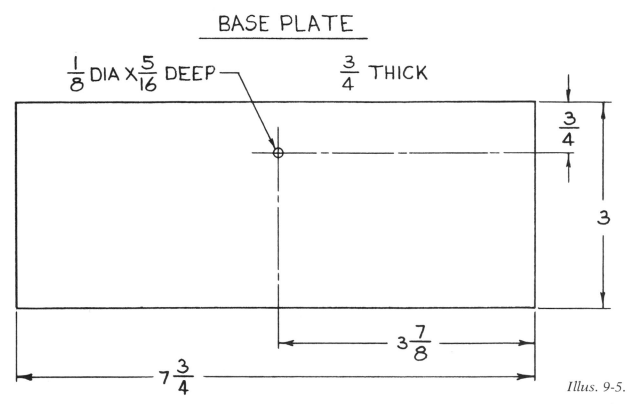

BASE PLATE

$\frac{1}{8}$ DIA X $\frac{5}{16}$ DEEP

$\frac{3}{4}$ THICK

$\frac{3}{4}$

3

$3\frac{7}{8}$

$7\frac{3}{4}$

*Illus. 9-5.*

161

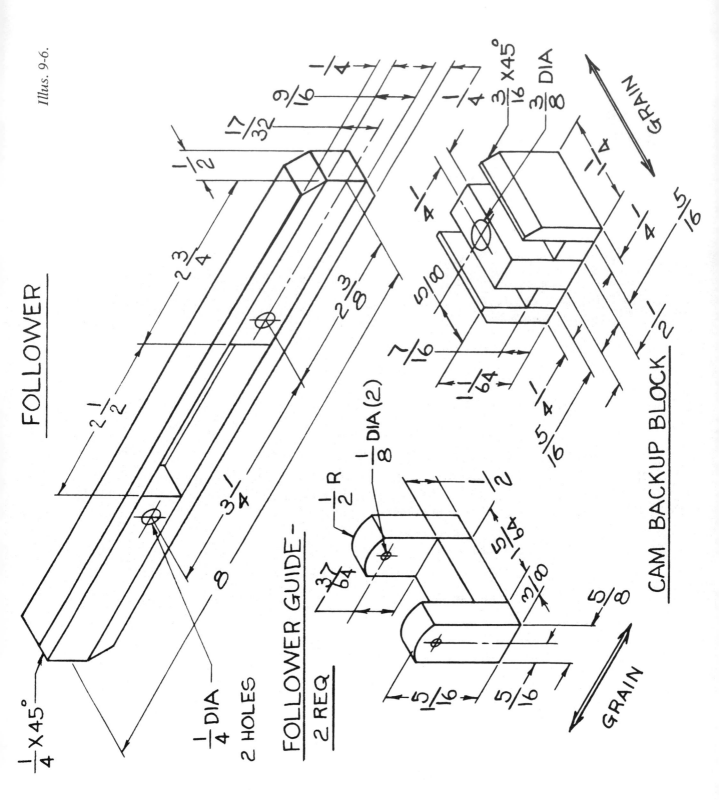

FOLLOWER

$\frac{1}{4}$ X 45°

$2\frac{1}{2}$

$2\frac{3}{4}$

$2\frac{3}{8}$

$\frac{1}{2}$

$\frac{17}{32}$

$\frac{9}{16}$

$\frac{1}{4}$

$3\frac{1}{4}$

8

$\frac{1}{4}$ DIA
2 HOLES

FOLLOWER GUIDE–
2 REQ

$\frac{1}{2}$ R

$\frac{1}{8}$ DIA (2)

$\frac{37}{64}$

$\frac{1}{2}$

$1\frac{5}{64}$

$\frac{3}{32}$

$\frac{5}{16}$

$\frac{5}{16}$

$\frac{5}{8}$

GRAIN

CAM BACKUP BLOCK

$\frac{3}{16}$ X45°

$\frac{3}{8}$ DIA

$1\frac{1}{4}$

$1\frac{1}{4}$

$\frac{5}{16}$

$\frac{1}{2}$

$\frac{1}{4}$

$\frac{5}{8}$

$\frac{7}{16}$

$1\frac{1}{64}$

$\frac{5}{16}$

$\frac{1}{4}$

GRAIN

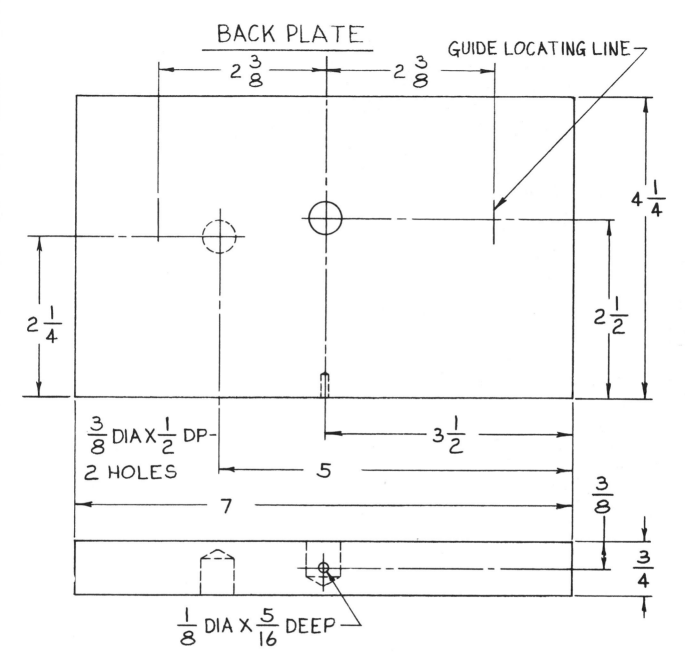

# BACK PLATE

Illus. 9-7.

163

*Illus. 9-8. The follower parts ready for gluing.*

*Illus. 9-9. Gluing together a blank for the follower guides.*

parts from rubbing, so check the assembly of your completed parts before trimming the block to its final height.

## Cam (Illus 9-10 and 9-11)

Check the size of your photocopy and glue the pattern to the stock. (See Illus. 9-12.) Drill the holes and saw and sand to the outline, but don't finish-sand until you have tried the cam in the assembled model.

## Remaining Parts (Illus. 9-13 and 9-14)

The two rollers are best made with a circle cutter, but if your cutter can't cut pieces this small, saw them out and sand them on a fixed pin, as explained in previous chapters.

All other parts are similar to those in earlier projects. If you cut both cams, you may want to make the handled retaining pin, shown as an alternate design in Illus. 9-14. Fit this so that it wiggles in and out easily, and orient

164

# 1 LOBE CAM PATTERN

GLUE TO $\frac{1}{2}$ INCH THICK STOCK

*Illus. 9-10.*

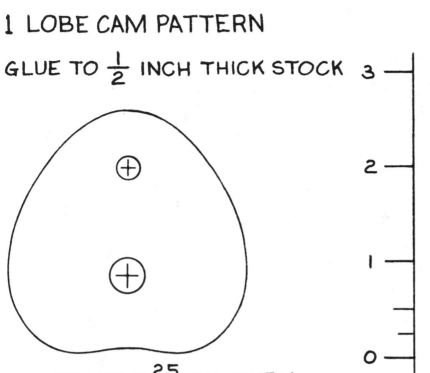

3 —

2 —

1 —

0 —

CENTER HOLE $\frac{25}{64}$ DIA THRU

HANDLE HOLE $\frac{1}{4}$ DIA X $\frac{3}{8}$ DEEP

# 3 LOBE CAM PATTERN

GLUE TO $\frac{1}{2}$ INCH THICK STOCK

*Illus. 9-11.*

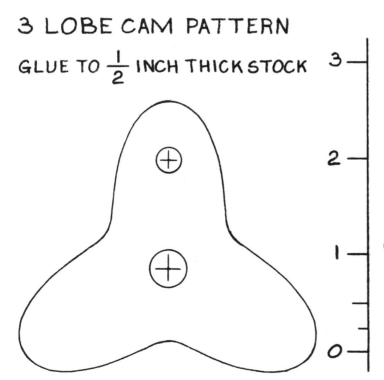

3 —

2 —

1 —

0 —

CENTER HOLE $\frac{25}{64}$ DIA THRU

HANDLE HOLE $\frac{1}{4}$ DIA X $\frac{3}{8}$ DEEP

*Illus. 9-12. The cam patterns glued to the wood.*

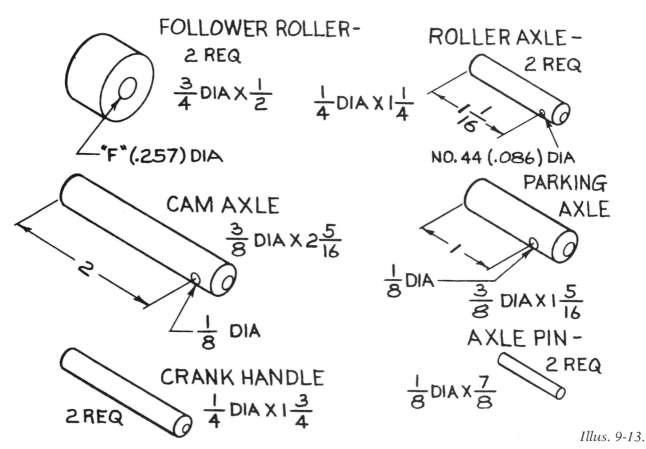

FOLLOWER ROLLER— 2 REQ

$\frac{3}{4}$ DIA X $\frac{1}{2}$

"F" (.257) DIA

ROLLER AXLE— 2 REQ

$\frac{1}{4}$ DIA X $1\frac{1}{4}$

$\frac{1}{16}$

NO. 44 (.086) DIA

CAM AXLE

$\frac{3}{8}$ DIA X $2\frac{5}{16}$

2

$\frac{1}{8}$ DIA

PARKING AXLE

$\frac{1}{8}$ DIA

1

$\frac{3}{8}$ DIA X $1\frac{5}{16}$

CRANK HANDLE

2 REQ

$\frac{1}{4}$ DIA X $1\frac{3}{4}$

AXLE PIN— 2 REQ

$\frac{1}{8}$ DIA X $\frac{7}{8}$

*Illus. 9-13.*

166

RETAINING PIN-
4 REQ
$\frac{1}{8}$ DIA X $\frac{5}{8}$

ROLLER AXLE PIN- 2 REQ
.086 DIA X $\frac{9}{16}$

PIN LIFTING HANDLE
2 REQ – GLUE PIN IN PLACE
BEFORE CUTTING PART FROM
LONG BLANK

DOWEL

$\frac{1}{8}$ DIA X $\frac{9}{16}$

the axle pin hole vertically, when using this design.

Fit the four slide-retaining pins so that they can be pushed in or out of engagement without a lot of force. (See Illus. 9-3.)

## ASSEMBLING THE MECHANISM

Shim the follower in the cam backup block, using equal amounts of cardboard and paper on each side, so that the part is centered in the block. Do the same for the two follower guides, although these shouldn't require much more than a piece of paper on each side to take up all clearance. Sand a piece of $\frac{3}{8}$-inch dowel about 5 inches long so that it fits easily in the backup block and the backplate. Push this through the two holes to dry-assemble the parts.

Measure from the baseplate to the follower at two widely separated points to establish the dimension for the levelling blocks. Select parallel blocks of scrap wood to fill the space so that the follower is levelled. Now remove the two guides and glue the backup block to the backplate, keeping the follower shimmed in place and levelled by the spacer blocks. Use the dowel for alignment, removing it before the glue sets up.

When the glue is dry, make small marks on the backplate to indicate the location of the follower guides. Shim these follower guides to the follower and glue them in place. (See Illus. 9-15.) Clean the assembly and glue in the cam axles, front and back, keeping the pin holes a little above the faces of the cams.

Glue the two roller axles into the follower slide. Now, set the follower in place, assemble the rollers, and try the cams for fit. They should have a little clearance at all points of rotation; so sand wherever there is not enough clearance. When the cams are satisfactory, fine-sand them and glue in their handles.

Clean all the parts and apply a finish. Wax all the bearing surfaces and assemble the components, checking each individually for smoothness of operation. This model is now ready to display. The three-lobed cam gives an especially lively action.

*Illus. 9-15. Gluing the follower guides to the backplate, using levelling blocks.*

*Illus. 9-16. The base and back subassembly.*

168

# Roller-Gearing Mechanism

This is an economical, low-friction alternative to conventional toothed gearing. It has been used to drive machine tables and heavy fixturing, as it is compact, requires less lubrication than ordinary gears, and can be built as strong as required for a given application. Its only drawback is that it is limited to a 1 to 2 speed ratio.

## HOW THE MECHANISM WORKS

The rule of hypocycloids tells us that if a small circle is rolled around the inside of a circle exactly twice as large in diameter, any point on the small circle will trace a straight line, which will be a radius line of the large

*Illus. 10-1. The Roller-Gearing mechanism.*

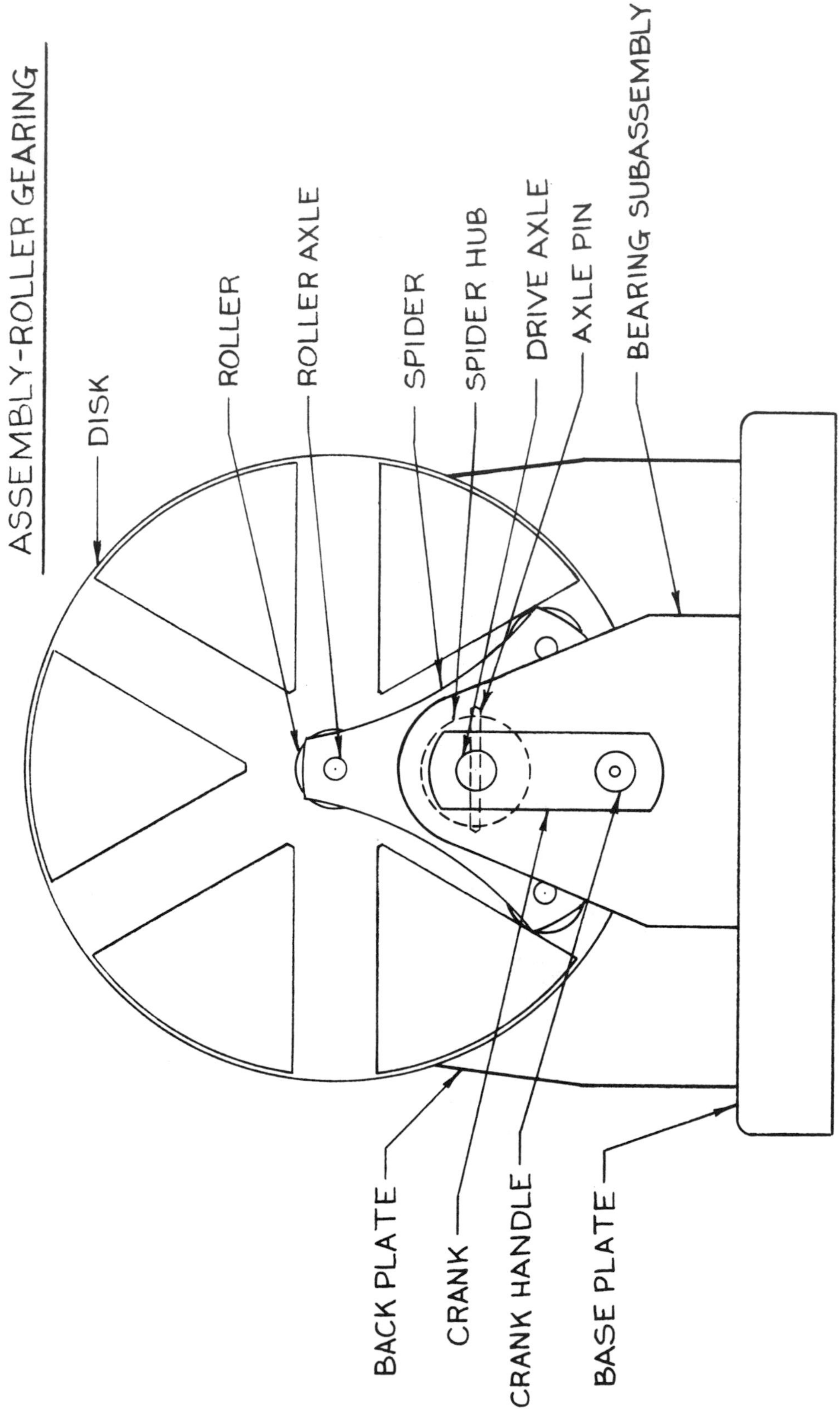

ASSEMBLY-ROLLER GEARING

DISK

ROLLER

ROLLER AXLE

SPIDER

SPIDER HUB

DRIVE AXLE

AXLE PIN

BEARING SUBASSEMBLY

BACK PLATE

CRANK

CRANK HANDLE

BASE PLATE

Illus. 10-2.

170

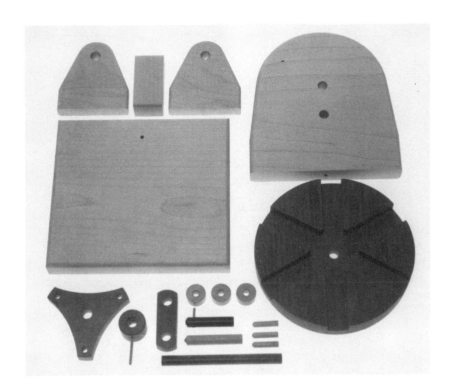

circle. If, then, you make two disks, one of which has rollers located on the circumference of the small circle, each of which is centered in a radial slot in the large disk, the two disks will operate together at uniform velocity, with a ratio of 1 to 2 for any of the possible combinations of rollers and slots.

## MAKING THE PARTS

### The Disk (Illus. 10-5)

Draw a five-inch-diameter circle on the material, keeping it slightly away from the

*Illus. 10-4. The triangular blank laid out.*

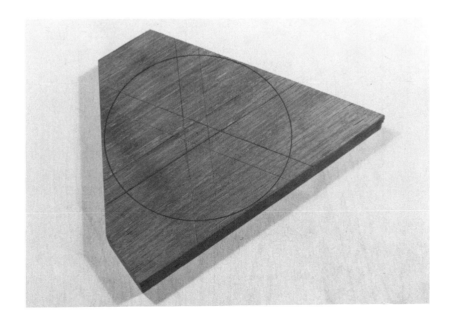

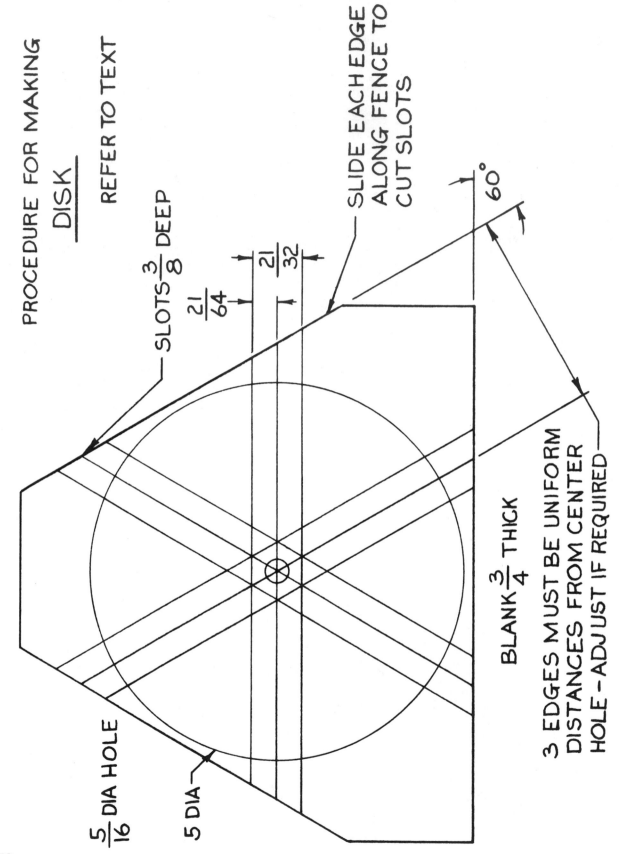

PROCEDURE FOR MAKING
DISK
REFER TO TEXT

SLOTS $\frac{3}{8}$ DEEP

$\frac{21}{64}$

$\frac{21}{32}$

SLIDE EACH EDGE
ALONG FENCE TO
CUT SLOTS

60°

$\frac{5}{16}$ DIA HOLE

5 DIA

BLANK $\frac{3}{4}$ THICK

3 EDGES MUST BE UNIFORM
DISTANCES FROM CENTER
HOLE – ADJUST IF REQUIRED

172

*Illus. 10-5.*

edges. Lay out two 60-degree angles to form an equilateral triangle, equally spaced from the circle. Extra flats on the corners won't matter as long as they aren't too large. Cut out the triangle and check the angles with a good protractor, correcting any errors with a small plane. It is important that the triangle is an accurate 60 degrees on each side. (See Illus. 10-4.)

Set a marking gauge to the centerline dimension and draw a short line parallel to each of the three sides. These lines will probably intersect to form a tiny triangle. Drill a 5/16-inch-diameter hole as accurately centered in this triangle as possible. Put the drill shank or other rod in the hole and measure from it to each side of the triangle. If there is a noticeable difference in the measurements, correct it before proceeding.

Set a marking gauge to the location of one side of a slot and draw lines that are parallel to each side of the triangle. Repeat this for the other side of the slot. Carefully mark one set of the lines around the corners onto the edges of the blank, to aid in setting up the slotting operation.

Now, cut the slots with a table saw, or on a router table. You can use either a sharp circular saw blade or sharp router bit. A circular saw blade will not chip the blank as much, but a router bit makes the smoothest, most accurate cut. However you cut the slots, work up to a finished depth and width in easy stages. You will undoubtedly experience some chipping of the sharp points at the inner ends of the slots. This will not noticeably affect operation, so just trim them neatly to a uniform dimension, using a sharp chisel. (See Illus. 10-6.)

Saw the outside diameter, and belt- or disk-sand it to size on a fixed pin. (See Illus. 10-7.) Chamfer the back of the disk on the router table as described for the Intermittent Drive in Chapter Eight. The front face has too many corners to risk a machining operation, so use a sharp block plane and/or a sanding block to form a uniform chamfer. Sand everything smooth, and lightly round the sharp corners of the slots.

*Illus. 10-6. The slots cut on the blank.*

*Illus. 10-7. Belt-sanding the out-side diameter of the disk.*

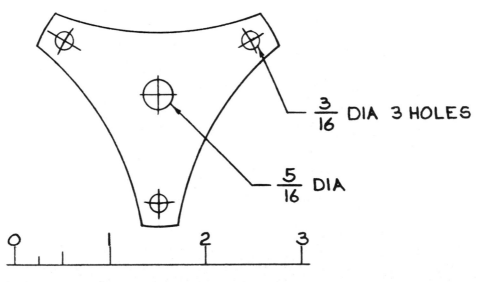

PATTERN FOR

SPIDER

GLUE TO $\frac{3}{8}$ STOCK

$\frac{3}{16}$ DIA 3 HOLES

$\frac{5}{16}$ DIA

0    1    2    3

*Illus. 10-8.*  INCH SCALE TO CHECK PHOTOCOPY

174

## Spider

Use the pattern in Illus. 10-8 to make this part, checking the size of the photocopy. The hub is easily made with a circle cutter, but if yours cannot cut a piece this small, just saw the part and sand it smooth.

## Rollers (Illus 10-11)

I make the rollers with a circle cutter that will cut down to a ⁷⁄₁₆ inch diameter. If you don't have such a tool, drill the parts, saw them to their outlines, and sand them to size on a fixed pin. It is important that these little parts are concentric, so make sure that you make them as accurately as possible. (See Illus. 10-10.)

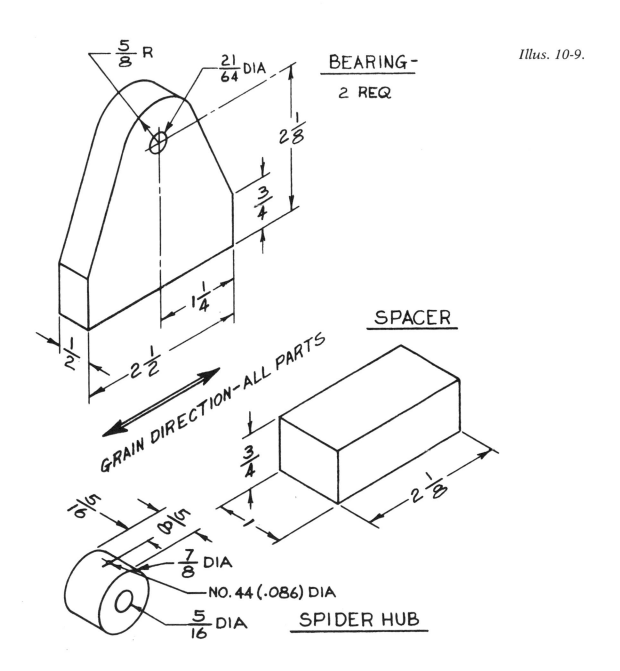

*Illus. 10-9.*

BEARING - 2 REQ

SPACER

SPIDER HUB

175

*Illus. 10-10. The small rollers on the blank.*

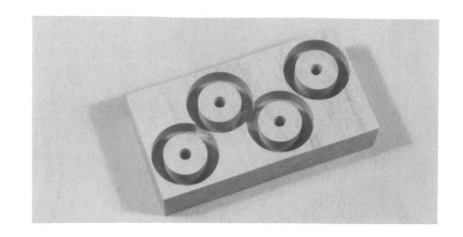

*Illus. 10-11.*

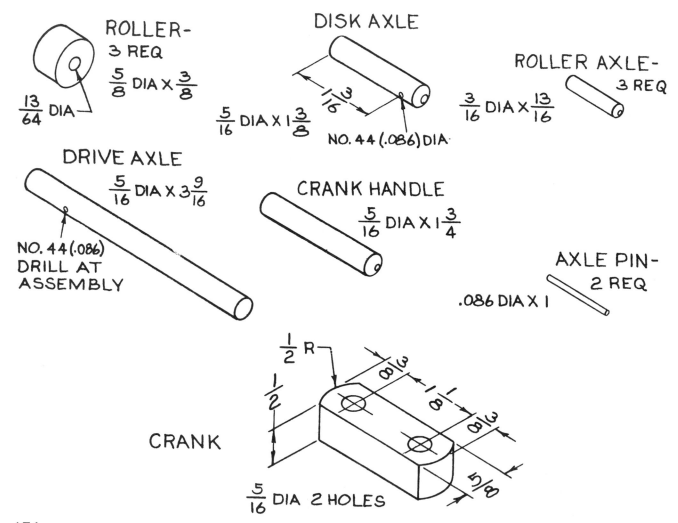

ROLLER-
3 REQ
$\frac{5}{8}$ DIA X $\frac{3}{8}$
$\frac{13}{64}$ DIA

DISK AXLE
$\frac{3}{16}$
$\frac{5}{16}$ DIA X $1\frac{3}{8}$
NO. 44 (.086) DIA

ROLLER AXLE-
3 REQ
$\frac{3}{16}$ DIA X $\frac{13}{16}$

DRIVE AXLE
$\frac{5}{16}$ DIA X $3\frac{9}{16}$
NO. 44 (.086)
DRILL AT
ASSEMBLY

CRANK HANDLE
$\frac{5}{16}$ DIA X $1\frac{3}{4}$

AXLE PIN-
2 REQ
.086 DIA X 1

CRANK
$\frac{1}{2}$ R
$\frac{1}{2}$
$\frac{3}{8}$
$1\frac{1}{8}$
$\frac{3}{8}$
$\frac{5}{8}$
$\frac{5}{16}$ DIA 2 HOLES

## Remaining Parts (Illus. 10-11–10-13)

Size the roller axles to fit easily into their holes in the spider, to prevent this slender part from splitting.

The backplate, baseplate, crank, and bearing blocks are straightforward, except for one detail: the lower of the two holes in the backplate is used to align the bearings at assembly. When you have drilled the parts, assemble the two bearings and the backplate on a dowel, orienting the grain on all three parts so that they can be planed in the same direction. Clamp the parts together and level their lower edges with a sharp plane so that the axle holes will be a uniform height from the baseplate.

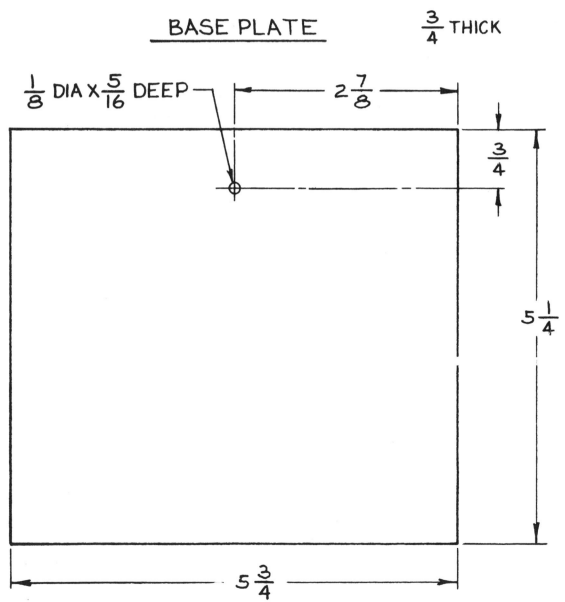

BASE PLATE $\frac{3}{4}$ THICK

$\frac{1}{8}$ DIA X $\frac{5}{16}$ DEEP

$2\frac{7}{8}$

$\frac{3}{4}$

$5\frac{1}{4}$

$5\frac{3}{4}$

*Illus. 10-12.*

177

# BACK PLATE

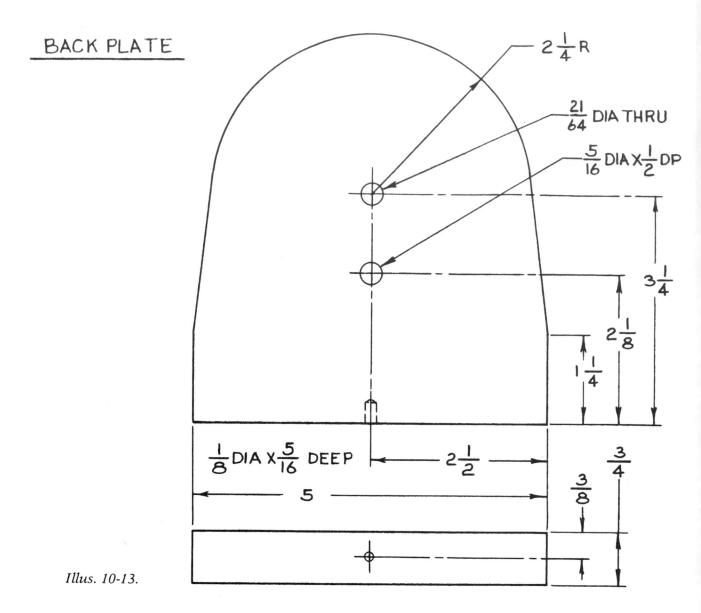

$2\frac{1}{4}$ R

$\frac{21}{64}$ DIA THRU

$\frac{5}{16}$ DIA X $\frac{1}{2}$ DP

$3\frac{1}{4}$

$2\frac{1}{8}$

$1\frac{1}{4}$

$\frac{1}{8}$ DIA X $\frac{5}{16}$ DEEP

$2\frac{1}{2}$

$\frac{3}{4}$

$5$

$\frac{3}{8}$

*Illus. 10-13.*

## Assembling the Mechanism

Put a dowel through the two bearings and glue them onto the spacer block. When it is dry, scrape or file the bottom of this subassembly to a flat surface. (See Illus. 10-14.) Glue the hub to the spider, aligning the grain and using a waxed dowel to center the parts. Glue in the roller axles so that they extend 3/8 inch from the face of the spider.

Clean out the hole with a drill, if necessary, and slide in the drive axle so that it is flush with the face of the spider. Mark both parts for future assembly, and drill the pin hole

through the axle. Push in the pin, assemble the axle into the bearings, and glue the crank onto its other end, allowing a little operating clearance. When dry, drive out the pin, remove the axle, and sand the end flush with the crank. Glue in the crank handle.

Glue the backplate to the base. Attach the disk axle to the disk, so that the pin hole is just clear of the backplate, and sand it flush with the bottom of the slot when it is dry.

Cut a piece of scrap to 1 25/32 inches to use as a spacer. A word of caution: if the disk is thicker than 3/4 inch or the axle projects more than 1 inch from the disk, you will have to

178

*Illus. 10-14. Gluing the bearing subassembly.*

*Illus. 10-15. Gluing the bearing to the base.*

increase the size of the assembly spacer to compensate for this.

Put a piece of dowel through both bearing holes, apply glue to the lower surface of the bearings, set the assembly spacer in place, and then carefully lower the bearings into position, sliding the dowel into the hole in the backplate. Clamp the parts, removing the spacer when you are certain that nothing will move. (See Illus. 10-15.)

Apply a finish and wax all the moving parts. Assemble the disk to the backplate. Put the rollers on their axles, set them in the slots, and turn the disk to bring the spider in line with its driving axle. Slide the axle into the spider, checking the alignment marks, and push in the axle pin. The unit should operate smoothly. This model gets a great deal of attention from visitors.

# CHAPTER 11

# Workshop Aids

The workshop aids featured in this chapter will prove particularly useful when you are making the projects in this book, but will also be helpful on other woodworking jobs or projects. They are easy to make and will prove indispensable for small work.

## AN IMPROVED WEDGE VISE

If you plane small parts with hand planes, you know how difficult it is to hold these pieces in a conventional vise. The wedge vise shown Illus. 11-1–11-5 is my version of an ancient tool, modified to handle very small work. It will clamp parts up to 2 inches in thickness. An integral sliding key prevents the wedge from lifting; when the wedge is slid all the way to the left, it is locked in place for storage and won't be lost. (See Illus. 11-1.)

My vise was built with two projecting tangs, to engage the dog slots in my workbench. You can also screw one of these vises to the bench top, as many people do, or glue on a downward-projecting plate to clamp the vise to the bench apron.

To make the vise, select a very tough and dry wood; the wedge vise shown here is made of red oak. Plane this to its final thickness. A thickness of ¾ inch is nominal; you can make it thicker or thinner. Lay out the parts and cut them to size. The 19-degree angle was experimentally determined as the best compromise between good holding ability and a relatively quick release, and should be maintained. It is also important that the clamping surfaces on the wedge be parallel with the one on the fixed jaw. The ¼-inch-thick key

and its keyway are centered in the ¾-inch thickness of the parts, and should fit closely. Glue the two parts of the main body, drawing them tight with the reinforcing bolts. When they are dry, check the assembly for flatness, correcting it if necessary.

If your bench has the dog slots, cut the mortises as shown and insert two tight-fitting tangs, adjusting the dimensions as needed so that the wedge vise will fit your workbench.

My vise has a Danish oil finish, which I periodically renew. Whatever you use, resist the temptation to wax anything, or your vise won't clamp on the work.

I believe you will find this tool quicker and handier than a regular vise, and much kinder to fragile parts.

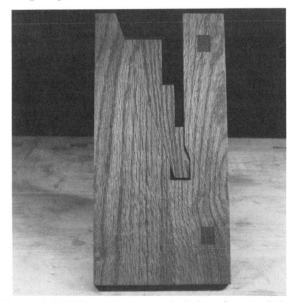

*Illus. 11-1. When the integral sliding key is slid all the way to the left, the wedge is locked in place for storage.*

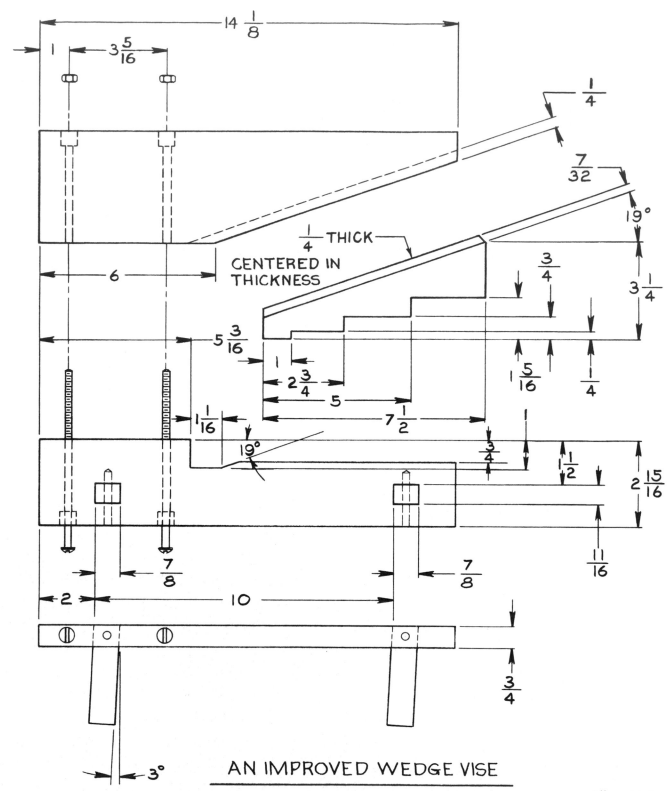

$14\frac{1}{8}$

$1$  $3\frac{5}{16}$  $\frac{1}{4}$

$\frac{7}{32}$

$19°$

$\frac{1}{4}$ THICK
CENTERED IN
THICKNESS

$6$

$3\frac{1}{4}$

$5\frac{3}{16}$  $\frac{3}{4}$

$1$  $\frac{1}{4}$

$2\frac{3}{4}$  $1\frac{5}{16}$

$5$

$7\frac{1}{2}$

$1\frac{1}{16}$  $19°$  $\frac{3}{4}$  $1\frac{1}{2}$  $2\frac{15}{16}$

$\frac{7}{8}$  $\frac{7}{8}$  $\frac{11}{16}$

$2$  $10$

$\frac{3}{4}$

$3°$

## AN IMPROVED WEDGE VISE

*Illus. 11-2.*

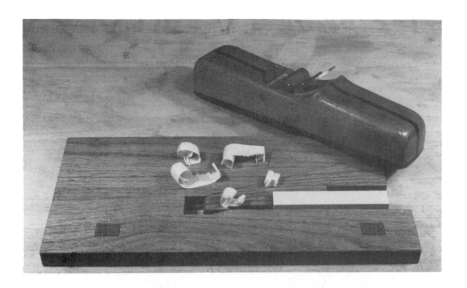

*Illus. 11-3. The vise in use.*

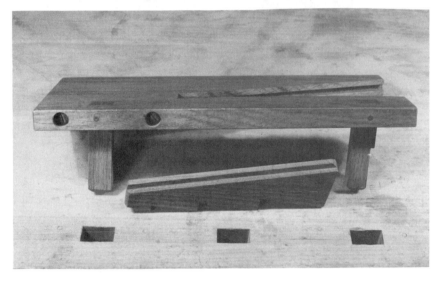

*Illus. 11-4. The vise and wedge, showing the key and keyway.*

*Illus. 11-5. The assembled wedge vise.*

## WOODEN CLAMPS

You have probably noted the sizes of unique wooden clamps that appear in some of the photos of this book. These are copies of a set of steel clamps I saw in a fellow's tool chest a long time ago. You can make these clamps just about any size desired for a fraction of the cost of a conventional carpenter's hand screw. As both of the screws project from the same jaw, the clamp will fit in places where others can't be used.

For large version of these clamps, use threaded rod. The smaller ones are built around long bolts. Any time I see long screws that have threads running throughout their full length, I buy them to use for making clamps.

The smallest of the three clamps featured here, which is shown in Illus. 11-6 and 11-7, is the one most used on the projects in this book. It has a clamping capacity of 4 inches, and can be adjusted very quickly, because it is built with free-spinning knurled nuts. The clamp is built around ¼–20 × 6-inch button-head machine screws. If you acquire other hardware, you must adjust the drawing dimensions to suit.

Cut the jaws to the drawing dimensions in Illus. 11-6 from strong, straight-grained wood. Drill the 5⁄16-inch clearance holes in the movable jaw, and spot them into the fixed jaw. Drill the two holes in the fixed jaw with a 3⁄16-inch drill, and thread them with a ¼-20 tap; this will provide a tight fit for the screws. The steps on the insides of the jaws at the rear provide clearance for the clamping nut and

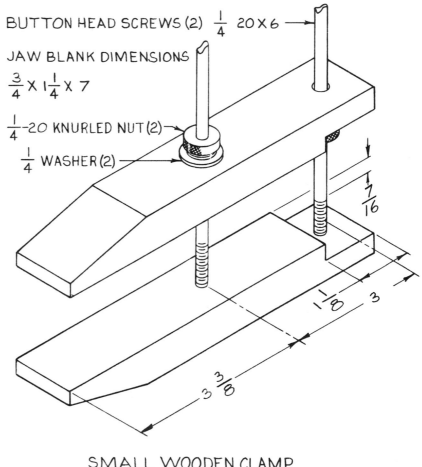

BUTTON HEAD SCREWS (2) $\frac{1}{4}$ 20 × 6

JAW BLANK DIMENSIONS
$\frac{3}{4}$ × $1\frac{1}{4}$ × 7

$\frac{1}{4}$-20 KNURLED NUT (2)

$\frac{1}{4}$ WASHER (2)

$\frac{7}{16}$

$1\frac{1}{8}$   3

$3\frac{3}{8}$

SMALL WOODEN CLAMP

*Illus. 11-6.*

*Illus. 11-8. The large clamp.*

allow the clamp to close all the way. If you don't need your clamp to close this far, eliminate these steps.

If you care to elongate the holes in the movable jaw to ⅜ inch, you will be able to clamp parts at about a 10-degree angle.

Apply an oil finish or something similar, and allow it to dry. Drive both screws into the fixed jaw until the heads are firmly seated. Now, assemble the movable jaw and the nuts and washers.

To use the clamp, run the nuts down until both jaws engage the work and are parallel to it. Now, tighten the center nut. Turn the rear nut upward, to increase the clamping force. If you want a more powerful clamp, like the intermediate-size clamp shown in Illus. 11-7, you can increase the distance between screws, leaving the front dimension as it is. The force exerted by these clamps is a direct function of the lever arm ratios, and the effort applied. For very strong clamps, make a deep cross-section like that on the large model in Illus. 11-8, and tighten it with a wrench.

To build the larger clamps shown in Illus. 11-7, screw threaded rod into tapped holes, drill cross-holes through the jaw and the screws, and drive in pins cut from brass rod.

A rod 36 inches long will, when cut in two, give the clamp a capacity of 14¾ inches. The clamp shown in Illus. 11-8 uses ⁵⁄₁₆-inch carriage bolts 8 inches long, also pinned in place, but will only close down to ½ inch. For really large models, you can buy quick-acting hand knobs from Reid Tool Supply Company, 1518 E. Katella Avenue, Anaheim, CA 92805. They are available in sizes from ¼ to ¾ inch, and permit a large clamp to be adjusted through its full range in a few seconds.

Try making a set of these clamps; you can't get anything as handy for so small an outlay of money and effort.

These clamps were first described in the No. 63, March/April 1987 issue of *Fine Woodworking* magazine.

## SANDING BLOCKS

For the odd sanding jobs such as removing fuzz, blending small radii, and general touching up small parts, a collection of ready-to-use sanding blocks and sticks is very helpful. While you can buy some similar items nowadays, most of these sanders can be made very cheaply and tailored to suit your particular requirements. The following instructions are for making some of my favorite tools.

The rectangular blocks shown in Illus. 11-9

each accept one-quarter sheet of sandpaper. Both blocks were originally made to use wood screws for clamping. After 10 years of use, the screws in one block stripped the wooden threads, which were then drilled out to take threaded brass inserts, and fitted with flathead machine screws. The other block still has its wood screws. You may use either system; if using wood screws select a very hard wood, so that the block will be durable.

It's best to work up a piece of stock long enough to make several blocks; this eliminates the danger of working short pieces, and you will have two or more sanders to use. Plane the material to the thickness and width shown in Illus. 11-10. If you need to use thinner or thicker wood, you will have to revise the width so that the tool still takes a quarter sheet of sandpaper. Remove the waste material in the center using either a table saw or a table-mounted router with straight and angled cutters. Round the corners, and then cut the blocks to length; sand them smooth.

Now, make a length of material for the clamps, and cut the clamps to length. Lay out the hole centers on each clamp, and drill and countersink for the screws. Use each clamp as a drill jig to mark the hole locations in its block. Mark each sandpaper clamp and its block, so that they are always assembled the same way that they were drilled.

*Illus. 11-9. Two rectangular sanding blocks, one with wood screws, one with threaded inserts.*

186

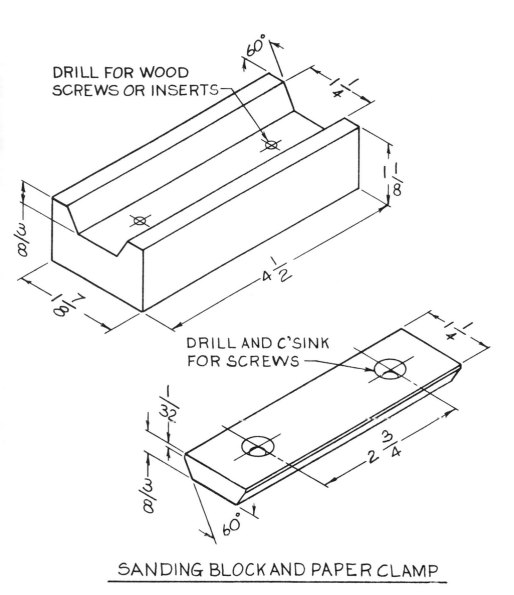

DRILL FOR WOOD
SCREWS OR INSERTS

60°

$4\frac{1}{2}$

$1\frac{1}{8}$

$\frac{3}{8}$

$1\frac{7}{8}$

DRILL AND C'SINK
FOR SCREWS

$1\frac{1}{4}$

$\frac{1}{32}$

$2\frac{3}{4}$

$\frac{3}{8}$

60°

SANDING BLOCK AND PAPER CLAMP

If you use certain threaded inserts, you may have to shorten them to stay within the thickness of your material.

Apply a coat or two of finish, and when it is dry, try loading the sandpaper. Set the block in the center of the long dimension of a quarter-sheet; fold the sheet around the block and into the center, holding the paper tightly. Set the clamp in place and tighten the screws to a light, uniform torque. Your sander is ready to use. I keep 100 grit on one block and 150 on the other, for the work I do.

## A Double-Grit Sanding Bar

This tool is somewhat like a single-grit version that has recently come on the market, but I have built these for over 30 years, and I think mine are more useful. If you use abrasive cloth from a roll, you can make these tools any length that you wish. If you want to use strips cut from sandpaper sheets, you are limited to a length of 9½ inches.

Plane stock for the body of the tool. The dimensions are quite flexible; however, the minimum thickness will be determined by your threaded inserts. I like to use 1/4-20 screws, and the inserts for these are enormous.

Illus. 11-12 shows dimensions for the sanding bar shown in Illus. 11-11, and you can modify them as required. Lay out the angled cut-outs for the clamps. I cut these on the table saw, using either a tenoning jig, or a wide, square-edged piece of stock to push the stick squarely through the cut. Make all the angle cuts first; then set the blade vertical and cut away the center waste material, using a succession of cuts. Round the corners; then lay out and drill for the hardware.

The clamps are easily made on the table saw; shape one clamp on each end of the block at least 5 inches long. Drill the holes before sawing them to length. Finish the parts, assemble the threaded inserts, and load your abrasive. Insert the ends of both strips under one clamp and gently tighten it. Work the free ends of the strips under the other clamp. Get the strips as taut as you can, and tighten the clamp.

Now return to the first clamp; loosen it, and pull the strips taut again before tightening the clamp. This aligns the abrasive strips with the body of the tool. I usually keep 100-grit cloth on one side, and 180-grit cloth on the other.

## A Tapered Sanding Block

This tool is designed to accept a strip cut the long way from a standard sheet of sandpaper. It's thin end permits sanding in otherwise inaccessible locations. Instead of threaded inserts being used in a small space, a hardwood dowel set into the block gives properly oriented grain directions for the wood screws, as they don't work too well in end grain.

Square-up a piece of material for the block; then lay out and drill the 3/8-inch hole for the dowel. Mark the dowel, so that it can be reassembled in the correct orientation. Then drill two 7/64-inch-diameter holes through the dowel and into the block to the depth shown in Illus. 11-13. Remove the dowel and open the holes in the block to 13/64-inch, to provide clearance for the screws.

Now, lay out the clearance cut for the paper clamp and cut it to size on the table saw. Last of all, lay out the profile of the block, cut it out on a band saw, and sand it to shape. At this time you may want to try a strip of sandpaper, to check whether the perimeter of your block is the right length, or whether you need to remove more material.

Square-up a block about 5 inches long, and lay out the clamp on one end of it. Drill the holes for the screws. If your drill wanders far from the proper location, as drills will do in

*Illus. 11-11. The double-grit sanding bar, disassembled.*

188

# DOUBLE-GRIT SANDING BAR

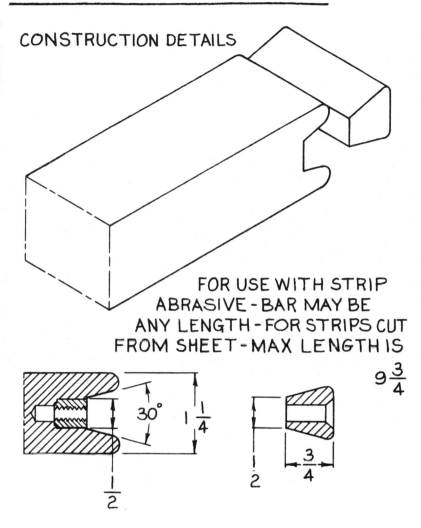

CONSTRUCTION DETAILS

FOR USE WITH STRIP
ABRASIVE - BAR MAY BE
ANY LENGTH - FOR STRIPS CUT
FROM SHEET - MAX LENGTH IS

$9\frac{3}{4}$

$30°$  $1\frac{1}{4}$

$\frac{1}{2}$

$2$  $\frac{3}{4}$

DETAILS FOR ONE END OF BAR - SEE TEXT

end grain, try again at the other end of the blank. When the holes are satisfactory, countersink them to bring the screw heads just about flush with the surface. Now, cut the part from the blank and sand it smooth.

Apply the finish to all parts. I don't glue in the dowel, so if the threads wear out, I can replace them. Cut a strip of sandpaper parallel to the long dimension of the sheet, center the thin end of the block in the strip, and fold the ends around and under the clamp. Pull the paper as tight as you can, while tightening the two screws. Be careful here—a 20-degree wedge is powerful enough to split the block if you get careless with the screwdriver. As it is, you will find it necessary to pry the wedge free each time the screws are loosened.

## Simple Sanding Sticks

I discovered a simple way to replace the sandpaper on a sanding stick. Spray several

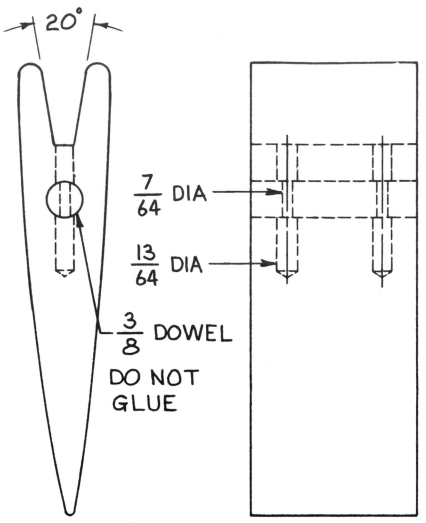

20°

$\dfrac{7}{64}$ DIA

$\dfrac{13}{64}$ DIA

$\dfrac{3}{8}$ DOWEL

DO NOT
GLUE

USE 2$\dfrac{1}{4}$ NO. 10 FLAT-HEAD SCREWS

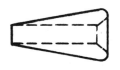 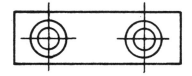

PATTERNS FOR

TAPERED SANDING BLOCK AND CLAMP

*Illus. 11-13.*

successive wet coats of 3-M 77 adhesive on a stick, allowing a few minutes drying time between coats. You can remove the sandpaper stuck in place when it is worn out by warming the stick with a heat gun, until the paper lifts off easily. Apply another piece of sandpaper while the stick is still warm, and it will adhere without additional adhesive. I usually get 2 to 3 renewals per stick, before having to respray. Mask the handle portion of the stick with newspaper taped in place, while spraying.

# INDEX